MAN AT PLAY

MAN AT PLAY

HUGO RAHNER, S.J.

HERDER AND HERDER

1967
HERDER AND HERDER NEW YORK
232 Madison Avenue, New York 10016

Chapters I–IV were first published under the title "Der spielende Mensch" in the *Eranos-Jahrbuch* of 1949, copyright 1949 by Rhein-Verlag. Chapter V was originally titled "Eutrapelie, eine vergessene Tugend," copyright 1963 by Hugo Rahner. Translated by Brian Battershaw and Edward Quinn.

Nihil obstat: John M. T. Barton, Censor Deputatus
Imprimatur: Patrick Casey, Vicar General,
Archdiocese of Westminster
December 9, 1964

Library of Congress Catalog Card Number: 67–14147
© 1965 by Burns & Oates
Printed in the United States

OTHER BOOKS BY HUGO RAHNER

SAINT IGNATIUS LOYOLA: LETTERS TO WOMEN
(Editor)

PRAYERS FOR MEDITATION
(With Karl Rahner)

Contents

Preface

PLAY should interest our contemporary world more than perhaps it does. Not only in the United States, but all over the world man today is much concerned with freedom, and the world of play is the world of freedom itself—of activity for its own sake, of spontaneity, of pure realization. Today, however, we seldom associate freedom with play. Freedom is grim—something to be fought for, something that we feel may confront us with antagonisms and even hatred instead of generating effusiveness and spontaneity and joy.

This pugnacious understanding of freedom has been with us ever since freedom became a "cause" at the opening of the modern age, and it of course can be explained. But, with or without explanation, it tends to outlaw play, for if play has nothing to do with freedom, where can it lay hold on life? When set against freedom instead of being associated with it, play strikes us as inconsequential, beneath the adult's dignity, something one descends to or "indulges" in, something childish.

And yet play is at least the half of life. Play and work derive from the same source in man's life world. When the infant first begins to use the powers which are latent within him and by using them to develop them, is he working or playing? When he flexes his muscles, crows and coos to himself and others all day long, takes his first steps—is this *Spass* or *Ernst*, "fun" or "for real"? There is of course no way of saying, for it is both. And this is the situation, where play and work coincide, in which learning (and life itself) is maximal. Educators have known this and have tried to keep alive this initial situation or to recover it in the classroom, making learning "fun." The Latin term *ludus* encapsulates the initial infantile work-play situation: it means both play and school. Out of this initial undifferentiated activity the two activities of work and play are polarized—differentiated, but always in dependence on each other.

Work and play define one another by dialectical contrast. Certainly work is what is not play and play is what is not work. Yet only in a sense is this true. This is the way it is until you arrive at a peak situation, when suddenly everything is reversed: the best players in any game turn out to be the professionals, those for whom the game is in fact work, a means of livelihood, and the best workers in any field are those for whom their work is a kind of play—the mechanic whose job serves his desire to "tinker" with machines, the basic research engineer who is "playing around" with various possibilities for a huge industrial complex, the financier who "plays the market," the philosopher who likes to "play" with ideas.

It cannot be otherwise. For if work is truly human work, it is something for which man is fitted, something that he can do and do well, though it may exhaust him, cost him, take something out of him. Thus work is, like play, free in the sense that it truly comes from within, comes as a realization of human potential, as an effusion of activity spilling out from its immanent source. Work is an expression of freedom and joy. But this is what play itself is.

What then is the difference between work and play? Does work take more effort? Not necessarily at all, although it is more demanding in the sense that the worker is less free to determine when and where he will begin and end. But even here, only in a sense is this true. Certainly the player of a game is not free to start before the referee's signal, whereas the worker often is free to start his day ahead of time. The worker is generally far more free to continue past five o'clock than the player is to continue playing after the last whistle blows.

The difference is, of course, that in play the players set up or freely accept their own rules. In work, the rules are set by actuality itself, by "life," by the way things are. And yet even here the dialectical relationship of work and play asserts itself, for the rules in a game are made rigid in order precisely to make the play world an artificial imitation of the rigidity of actuality. The game must be serious, in its own way "for real," like life. The result is again paradoxical, for in a sense the rules of a game become more rigid than many of those in real life: no court administers the law so inflexibly as a referee administers the rules in an athletic event. The law itself gives a judge discretion far surpassing that of a sports official.

Play is imitation. It is "art." Yet for man art is essential for grasp of actuality. One learns what reality is through imitation. A little girl learns how to be a mother by "playing house." A teacher begins to teach when he first stands in front of a class and plays the teacher's role—"makes like" a teacher. There is no other way to learn how to work than to play at working. For man, imitation is the door leading into the real.

Thus when we look at the total field of human activity, the amount of play in it should hardly surprise us, although it does. Games are play (except insofar as they are a means of livelihood, too). Plays are play—but not really for the playwright or for the actor, both of whom work to produce a creation which is pure play only for the audience (although the audience often pays to see plays and thus puts into them a certain amount of work). All literature and art is of course play. Music is play. Ballet is play. Painting and sculpture are play. Much of architecture is play, though the play must be kept somewhat relevant or "functional." With the growing leisure afforded by technological society, we are going to have to make do with more play. This means we are going to have to take play more seriously.

When we turn to work activities to see which of them are mixed with play, we find they all are. We have always known this, in fact: life, we say, is a game. Moreover, the play element (to use Huizinga's term) in serious activity seems sure in one way or another to increase as the activity becomes more serious. The race of two great world powers into space, in its most serious aspects, is quite obviously play, stylized competition, *agonia*—this is why it is thought of all over the world as a "race," a sporting event. It is no accident that the most strenuous corporate technological effort which man has ever made coincides *in fact* with the activity which earlier man often *jokingly* imagined to be the most playful, the most pointless (play is aimed at nothing outside itself) of all activities, spontaneous to the point of being totally ridiculous: shooting for the moon.

Much of this we have learned from the insightful work of Johan Huizinga (a philologist who tried playing at being a social historian and philosopher, and of course succeeded), from F. J. Buytendijk, G. von Kujawa, and others. It should be obvious how apposite this literature of play could prove for Christian theology, which is concerned with a God who is good and thus "diffusive of himself," spontaneously and freely giving first existence and then redemption to his creatures, who are thus the result of his play—only not in any sinister sense but in a positive and constructive sense. *Miris modis di ludos faciunt homines,* reads Plautus' *Rudens,* "In strange ways the gods make sport of men"—a passage which Gloucester virtually quotes in *Lear,* "They kill us for their sport." These were the pagan gods. The one true God is no such God. His play is the giving of life, first by creation and then by redemption. "Though I walk in the midst of the shadow of death, I will fear no evil," sings the Psalmist, knowing that despite evil and suffering, God will somehow prevail. "I am come that they may have life and have it more abundantly."

In the present work Father Hugo Rahner has seized on the concept of play as a means whereby a historian of religion can explicate in a fresh way the freedom of the children of God, which is a participation in the freedom of God himself. God's activity toward and in all his creation is like that germinal, undifferentiated activity of the child, which is both work and play, both serious application and spontaneous activity for its own sake. Thus only those who "become as little children" can enter the kingdom of heaven. In the natural life of the child, however, the juncture of work and play is fragile and doomed: soon life will cleave in two, and work and play will drift apart, even though they never entirely lose contact with one another. With God such separation never comes. God's work is always play in the sense that it is always joyous, spontaneous, and completely free.

Here and there through earlier ages, in the Scriptures and elsewhere, this sense of play has entered into ascetic and devotional awareness. It has remained, however, for Father Rahner to pull together and interpret, with true historical imagination, what hitherto have been scattered, if often profound, observations. The thoughtful and, historically speaking, newly reflective love of play which this volume evinces speaks well and hopefully for our own age.

Saint Louis University   WALTER J. ONG, S.J.

MAN AT PLAY

Introduction

Run home to thy house and there withdraw thyself, play and do what thou hast a mind.

(Ecclus. 32. 15–16 [11–12]*

THE idea that moved me to work out this philosophy of "Man at Play" and the truth from which this philosophy derives its validity—was first provided by the genius of Thomas Aquinas. The text from Ecclesiasticus which I have set at the head of this little work was also used by Aquinas to accompany an opusculum of his own. In a bold flight of allegory Aquinas interprets the words as follows: "The cultivation of wisdom has this advantage that its practice is sufficient unto itself. In outward matters man needs the aid of many things. As far, however, as the contemplation of wisdom is concerned, the more he is confined to his own solitary company, the more effectively he works. That is why the wise man in the above text calls man home to himself. . . . 'And there play,' he says. Consider here how aptly the contemplation of wisdom is compared to play. There are two reasons for this, both of them found in the very essence of play: first, play gives pleasure, and in the contemplation of wisdom there is the most profound pleasure . . .; secondly, the activity of play is not directed towards some other end, but is sought for its own sake; and this also holds true in regard to the pleasures arising from the contemplation of wisdom. . . . Hence even Eternal Wisdom likens its joy to that of play:

* This translation is inspired by the German. It does not reproduce verbatim any known English version.—*Translator*.

I

'I was daily his delight, always making play before him'
(Prov. 8. 30)."[1]

Aquinas expounds his philosophy of play in the chapters
especially devoted to that subject in the *Summa Theologica*,
and it is a philosophy illuminated by a wonderfully
balanced humanism.[2] In those chapters he admits his
debt to the *Nicomachean Ethics* of Aristotle. Indeed in his
commentary on that work he had already designated the
eutrapelia (examined fully in Chapter V below), or
nimbleness of mind which enables a man to play, as the
sign of a nobly formed character and an essential attribute
of the human ideal.[3] For both Aristotle and Aquinas the
"eutrapelos" is the man who strikes the happy mean
between the "bomolochos", the inveterate "funny man",
the buffoon, and the "agroikos", the humourless boor
who never as much as smiles. Aristotle says: "Recuper-
ative rest and cheerful play seem to be necessary for life."[4]
Aquinas writes: "Therefore, unmitigated seriousness
betokens a lack of virtue because it wholly despises play,
which is as necessary for a good human life as rest is."[5]
In the *Summa Theologica* this piece of Greek wisdom is
given a place at the very heart of the Christian art of life.

Yet Aquinas knows that his debt is not merely to the
Stagirite. He is well aware that he owes much more to
the spiritual wisdom of the Fathers and monks of the

[1] Thomas Aquinas, *Expositio super Boethium*, "*De Hebdomadibus*" (ed..
P. Mandonnet, Paris, 1927, pp. 165f.).
[2] Thomas Aquinas, *Summa Theologica*, IIa IIae, qu. 168, art. 2–4. [Engl.
tr. by the English Dominicans, London, 1912.]
[3] Thomas Aquinas, *In decem libros Aristotelis*, "*Ad Nicomachum*" *Expositio*,
II, lect. 9, No. 353; IV, lect. 16, No. 854; VIII, lect. 2, No. 1566 (Turin,
1934).—Aristotle, *Ethica Nicomachea*, X, 6, 1176B; IV, 9, 1128A; II, 7,
1108A.
[4] Aristotle, *Eth. Nic.*, IV, 8, 11, 1128B.
[5] Thomas Aquinas, *Eth. ad Nic.*, IV, 16, 854.

primitive Church. For instance, we hear the voice of Augustine who, in his *De Musica*,[1] says that the truly wise man will now and then relax the tension of his mind and let its sharp edge be dulled, and Aquinas adds that it is just this that is achieved by playful action and speech.[2] And here Aquinas recalls the charming story of St John the Apostle which he had read in the *Collationes* of Cassian.[3] The story tells how in his old age the apostle would play with a partridge. This, in one Carolingian version, elicits the charming remark: "Nay, mark how this old man plays with a bird—just like a boy!"[4] Then there is that other strange story which St Thomas had read in the history of the monastic Fathers. It concerns the great Paphnutius and his humility before the hidden virtue of a flute-playing robber, whose ill-spent life he saw ending —in spite of everything—in heavenly bliss.[5]

It is this humane and Christian philosophy of man at play that is my subject here, and for us men and women of today some knowledge of it is a healing necessity, trapped as we are on the hopelessly wrong road of idiotic earnestness, or on the senseless one of exclusive pre-occupation with the things of this world. The best spirits of our time have bruised and bloodied themselves in grappling with this question or found release from it in laughter. When Hermann Hesse assumes the task, as he does in his *Glasperlenspiel* ("The Glass Bead Game"), of showing a civilization that is perishing in the barren solemnity of a purely utilitarian view of life—when Hesse sets out to show that civilization that a true and full

[1] Augustine, *De Musica*, II, 14 (*PL* 32, 1116A).
[2] Thomas Aquinas, *S. Th.*, IIa IIae, qu. 168, art. 2, Sed contra.
[3] Ibid., Corp.—Cassian, *Collationes*, 24, 21 (*PL* 49, 1313A ff.).
[4] Hincmar of Reims, *Vita Sancti Remigii*, 13 (*PL* 125, 1140f.).
[5] *Vitae Patrum*, VIII, 63 (*PL* 73, 1170f.).—Rufinus, *Historia Monachorum*, 16 (*PL* 21, 435f.).

human being must be a creature of light-hearted, care-free play, a creature whose play is filled with the spirit and is, for that very reason, serious play, then he acts as a true *ludimagister* (schoolmaster and master of play), and sets himself to face a problem which is among the most profound in our whole cultural and religious history. As is shown by the quotation from Albertus Secundus with which he prefaces his novel, he is seeking to bring home to us how, despite the putrid corruption of an age in which our lives are largely governed by the ephemeral stimuli of journalistic caprice, man can still attain a spiritual discipline of monastic severity by learning to turn his life into a game. It is a game in which the power and un-inhibited grace of the expert can only be reached by the man who, through painful and serious effort, has learnt to play it by "a continent and selfless life of absolute re-nunciation comparable to the strictly regulated and penitential lives led by those who take part in the exercises of St Ignatius".[1] A man of such Castalian lightness of heart can work everything into this wonderful game, the classical cadences of a "biblical text, a sentence from one of the Fathers or from the order of the Latin Mass, just as easily . . . as . . . a melody of Mozart's".[2] A man so formed would be a man whose spirit is truly free, a man released from the trammels of self and capable of com-plete self-surrender, a man whose disappointments have turned into fun, a man with the easy step of one who has the earth at his feet and who no longer—by taking them too seriously—disfigures any of the values of this world—a *Homo vere ludens*!

[1] Hermann Hesse, *Das Glasperlenspiel*, I, p. 59, Zurich, 1943. [Gesam-melte Werke, p. 50. Berlin, 1951.]
[2] Ibid., p. 61. [p. 52.]

The truth of which the author gives us a glimpse in his *Glasperlenspiel* is something of which the hidden sages among the Greeks and among the Fathers of the Christian Church had a much profounder knowledge, something which they saw to be directly related to a living, personal God; and my purpose in putting these few thoughts before you is to drive that truth home. I shall do this by producing a very great quantity of evidence, evidence which I have gathered from the treasuries of these, the greatest of our spiritual *ludimagistri*. My starting-point will be the last page of the work, *Homo Ludens*, by that great philosopher of civilization Johan Huizinga,[1] the page on which he just suggests that the loveliest things in the spiritual life of man are no more than imperfectly realized imitations of that Divine Wisdom which since the beginning of time makes play before the face of God. This is where I take up the thread, and what I am aiming at is a theological and religious interpretation of play. My object is to show, by drawing on the forgotten riches of antiquity and the ancient Church, what modern man has lost because this faculty of play has been lost to him. Lost because, to quote Elisabeth Langgässer, he has become a being without mystery and "a mere part of the ordered mass of termites of which one is indistinguishable from another."[2] The dying Father Benoît (a character in this thoughtful novel), who in his fever sees all the secret creeping sicknesses of our modern world, speaks words in his prayer to God which exactly express what I am seeking to convey by what I have written and by the

---

[1] Johan Huizinga, *Homo Ludens*, Amsterdam, 1938 [Engl tr.: *Homo Ludens. A Study of the Play-Element in Culture* (International Library of Sociology and Social Reconstruction), London, 1949.]

[2] Elisabeth Langgässer, *Das unauslöschliche Siegel*, p. 478, Hamburg, 1946.

5

illustrations that I have adduced: "Who will be converted
to thee, O my God? Who will again give to this land
monasteries of silence and adoration? Who will make
them feel again the need to play—even as the Divine
Wisdom made play at the beginning of time before the
world was made? Who will transform this hideous edifice
of unrelieved utility, O my uninhibited God, into one of
sheer, gratuitous uselessness? Who will turn every petition
into a pure song of praise, and every clamouring want into
a vessel overflowing with the generosity of the beginning?"

It will not be necessary to discuss here at any length
the great richness of that rather special kind of being
alive that we summarize with the word "play". That has
already been done by such men as Buytendijk,[1] Huizinga[2]
and von Kujawa[3]—by the last in the book he dedicated
to Jung. I will merely sketch out a few fundamental ideas
which as we proceed will gain a fuller content of meaning
—and of beauty. If I say that man with a true ability to
play is—or, alas, was—man at his highest level of cultural
development, I do so on the basis of a comprehensive
view of the thing we call play, a phenomenon which, in its
utterly simple wealth of form, is, like all dispositions of
the soul, almost incapable of description in so many
words. For play is a human activity which engages of
necessity both soul and body. It is the expression of an
inward spiritual skill, successfully realized with the aid of
physically visible gesture, audible sound and tangible
matter. As such it is precisely the process whereby the
spirit "plays itself into" the body of which it is a part.
In the biological sphere this is the kind of rhythmic,

---

[1] F. J. Buytendijk, *Wesen und Sinn des Spieles*, Berlin, 1933.
[2] Johan Huizinga, *Homo Ludens*.
[3] G. von Kujawa, *Ursprung und Sinn des Spiels*, Leipzig, 1940.

essentially beautiful exercise that forms the body; in the spiritual field it is art in the widest and most comprehensive sense of that term. And so we talk of play whenever the mastery of the spirit over the possibilities presented by the body has in some way attained its perfection, a perfection that shows itself in the easy agility, the shimmering elegance of some acquired skill; when word, sound or gesture has been made obedient and pliable to the spirit; when the physically visible has become the expression of an inner fullness that is sufficient to itself. Play is thus an activity that is undertaken for the sake of being active, meaningful but directed towards no end outside itself. The happily playing child, the virtuoso playing upon his instrument—and how few in fact really "play" upon it!—the genius whose work flows from his fingers with the effortless ease of one playing a game— all these are but realizations of man's deep-seated longing for a free, unfettered, eager harmony between body and soul.

It is at this point that we may begin to attempt a deeper and essentially theological interpretation of the concept of play and all that follows here is really inspired by that purpose. I will start by asking this question: How comes it that the child, the supreme and most obvious example of man at play, has been made the very symbol and personification of that life of blessedness, which we have lost and which we so ardently yearn to regain? Why is it that in every civilization religious men have symbolized the nature of life in the world to come under the form of a wonderfully carefree and supremely happy dance? The answer is to be sought in that hidden knowledge— the fruit of a primitive experience, confirmed by revelation—that our Creator had originally endowed us with a different and more finely attuned relation between body and soul than that which we now possess, and that our task is now to regain it, in suffering and in seriousness of purpose, to regain it though in doing so our lives are rent asunder. As C. G. Jung and K. Kerényi have shown,[1] these primitive intimations find expression in the myth of the playing infant god, and the *putti* of baroque art, who play so merrily with the globe of the earth, have behind them some vague awareness of all this, an awareness vehicled by the Christian truth that only "little children" will enter the kingdom of heaven. Play and dance, therefore, when they genuinely succeed in expressing here on earth what is in the heart, are an anticipation of heavenly joy. They are a kind of rehearsal, fashioned into gesture, sound or word, of that Godward directed harmony of body and soul which we call heaven. Eternity will in fact be what the Paradise we have lost was—a divine children's game, a dance of the spirit, and the soul's becoming flesh in a way that is at long last wholly and eternally perfect. Now we can understand why play was in its first beginning accounted a sacred thing, something dedicated to the Divinity, and why the dance was essentially a cultic act. The converse of this is also true. None of the things that give its unique character to this activity of human play—the light-hearted relaxing of the mind, the charm of a certain smiling contempt for mundane things, the wisdom of ease and detachment— none of these things, I say, is even possible unless man refrains from distorting the world into a thing whose reality lies wholly within itself, or even, for that matter, in his own mind. They only become possible when man's

[1] C. G. Jung and K. Kerényi, *Essays on a Science of Mythology*. The Myth of the Divine Child and the Mysteries of Eleusis (Bollingen Series, XXII), New York, 1949.

mind is open to God, when in the shaping of his life he has in some measure anticipated eternity. They only become possible if he, as it were, kicks the world away from him with the airy grace of a dancer, and yet, at the same time, presses it to his heart because God the Creator can himself be seen in its transparency.

The ideas which I have just sketched out fall into a sort of natural order which has determined the grouping and arrangement of a very great wealth of material, material made up out of the utterances by the great *ludimagistri*, Christian and pagan, on this subject of human play. Thus we cannot truly grasp the secret of *Homo ludens*, unless we first, in all reverence, consider the matter of *Deus ludens*, God the Creator who, one might say, as part of a gigantic game called the world of atoms and spirits into being; for not even the most inspired gesture of man at play can be other than a clumsy, childish imitation of the Logos, who, since the beginning of time, has made play before the face of the Father. This, then, is Chapter I. It is only after that that I shall discuss, in Chapter II, the playing of man, and here I shall attempt a kind of psychography of *Homo ludens*, an analysis of that attitude that is poised between gaiety and gravity, between mirth and tragedy, and which the Greeks designated by the inimitable expression: ἀνὴρ σπουδογέλοιος – the "grave-merry" man. Such a man is capable of making his life into a game, and a very lovely one at that, because he knows that this life is either a comedy or a tragedy. "Fun and gravity are sisters", says Plato in his Sixth Letter.[1] In Christian truth this apparent contradiction is resolved into that grave mirth from which the tragic is wholly absent and which led Clement of

[1] Plato, *Epistulae*, 6, 323D.

9

Alexandria to speak of life as a "divine children's game".

From this psychography of the Christian as a *Homo ludens* who has wholly freed himself from all vestiges of the tragic, my train of thought leads to a sublime region of theology, and, in this third chapter, my words and all their implications must be carefully weighed, lest I give the impression of seeking to rob the world of Christian truth of its tremendously serious quality. Actually I shall try—with the help of the Fathers and theologians—to say something of the playing of the Church, the *locus* of soul and body in which the Logos made man carries on his "game of grace"; the *locus* also where the truly Catholic man—that beautiful unity of grace and humanity, in so far as he has not lost himself in the omnipresent intellectualism of the day—answers the game of grace with his counter-play of liturgy and sacrament, so that Church, grace and liturgical action become for him no more than a prelude to that final carefree gaiety of heart which he will experience one day in the everlasting game of the Beatific Vision.

Finally, since no symbolic idea can better describe this great game which is of heaven and earth at once, than that of the heavenly dance, I shall conclude my *Theologia ludens*, in Chapter IV, with an attempted theological interpretation of the dance itself. In doing so, I take a glance at the inexpressible mysteries of the return to the play of pure radiance, of which Plato had had some faint intimation in the *Phaedrus*[1] and which the Christian Hippolytus of Rome in a kind of hymnal intoxication refers to as the eternal feast of the Logos, the feast in which the Logos is the leader of the mystical round-dance, as the dancing chorus of the earth returns to God.[2]

[1] Plato, *Phaedrus*, 250B.
[2] Cf. Hippolytus, *Homiliae in Pascha*, 6 (*PG* 59, 744D f.).

I

The Playing of God

PLATO refers to man as a παίγνιον θεοῦ – a plaything of God, and sees in this the highest perfection a creature can attain. There is real perception in this, for if the highest attainable form of human development consists in the possession of those qualities which we especially associate with the idea of play, a lightness and freedom of the spirit, an instinctively unerring command of the body, a certain neatness and graceful nimbleness of mind and movement, then—platonically speaking—it is precisely through such things as these that man participates in the divine, it is precisely in such things as these that he achieves the intuitive imitation and the still earth-bound recovery of an original unity he once had with the One and the Good. When, therefore, we speak of God the Creator "playing", there lies concealed in that phrase the metaphysical truth that the creation of the world and of man, though a divinely meaningful act, was by no means a necessary one so far as God himself was concerned.

The words "meaningful but not necessary" bring into focus the essential content of this idea of the playing of God, yet they do not detract in any way from the enormous seriousness of God's creative activity—for that act is too full of a most profound meaning to be anything but immensely serious—but we do, in so conceiving of it, avoid falsifying its quality or presenting it as an act which flowed from God's nature as a metaphysical necessity, as though God were in some way subordinate to his own works or, in some pantheistic sense, identical with them. The Creator is free. Out of the vast multiplicity of possible ones he calls one particular order into being. It is a choice of genius—if such an expression may be applied to God; there is genius in the order's design and his purpose in creating it is that through it and in it his wisdom and goodness may be made visible. The very manner in which all created being proceeds from the hand of the Creator, the hand that works so gently and yet with such power and such sureness of touch, is itself also the inner rhythm, the entelechy of creation, pregnant with the meaning that is creation's end. In this way a cosmic game is played before God, extending from the round of the stars and atoms to the gravely beautiful play of the spirit of man, and to that blessed dance into which are joined the spirits returning homeward to God. It is only after we have spoken in all reverence of *Deus ludens* that *Homo ludens* can be understood.

Let us begin with the famous words from Plato's *Laws* which ring out like the noble major theme of some great symphony. "I seek", says the great *ludimagister* of the Greek art of life, "I seek to expound the best way in which men can shape their lives, and in this I appear to myself to be like a shipbuilder who in laying down the keel already determines the shape of the whole ship. Like him, I am carrying out a kind of keel-laying when I seek correctly to determine what conduct and what attitude of mind will best help our little ship of life to steer past the rocks of this human existence. . . . What I would say is this: serious things must be treated seriously, but not those that are not serious. In deed and in truth, however, it is God who is worthy of all our deepest and most blessed seriousness. Man, on the other hand, is, as I remarked previously,[1] a plaything in the hand of God, and truly this is the best thing about him. Everyone, therefore, whether man or woman, must strive towards this end and must make of the noblest games the real content of their lives."[2]

I do not seek to minimize the secret melancholy that inspires the wise and aging Plato of the *Nomoi* in this his review of human nature. "As to the chief part of their souls, men are mere marionettes (θαύματα)," he continues, "for they have little part in the true nature of things." In this judgement, given with a kind of wry smile, Plato touches one of the deep secrets of the playing of man. Such words could only havē been spoken by a man who, looking upwards to God, the essence of all being, had seen earthly things in their true perspective and who, because of this, treated man and his fate with neither more nor less seriousness than that which a strange and wonderful plaything deserves.

This is made marvellously clear in the objection raised in the ensuing dialogue by the Spartan Megillos, a sober and essentially practical man—and here we are at the very heart of the paradox of play: "In that case, you make us out to be worse than we really are, my friend"; and the Athenian replies: "Do not be surprised, Megillos, but rather give me some credit for my remarks, for my words were due to the fact that I was regarding God. They came from the mood which I have described. You may indeed be right. The condition of mankind is not so bad and in some measure it deserves to be taken seriously." But anyone who is truly in earnest about God will not be able to treat man as though the whole meaning of all

[1] Plato, *Laws*, 644DE.   [2] Ibid., 803BC.

created things were comprised in him; and only the man who has grasped this transcendence inscribed in the very essence of participated, created being can truly "play", for he has laid hold of the mean between gravity and fun, between the tragedy of existence and the light-hearted surrender to the game of life which is mysteriously guided by the goodness of a Wisdom itself also at play.

The sages of Greece had an intimation of all this which they showed in their myths and their philosophy. In a fragment of Heraclitus which various people have interpreted in various ways, this idea finds expression: "αἰὼν πατς ἐστι παίζων, πεττεύων. Παιδὸς ἡ βασιληίη – the Aeon is a child at play, playing draughts. The kingly rule is as a child's." [1] Nietzsche[2] tried his hand at finding a meaning for this passage from Heraclitus the Obscure, in which we would probably not be far wrong in seeing some distant echo coming from the depths of Orphic piety.[3] One feels in these words an understanding of the never-ending growth and decline of the cosmos which is "like a drink composed of mixed ingredients that disintegrates into its constituent elements unless it is from time to time stirred up"—[4] we feel the flux of all things. And yet behind the veils of appearances he who is truly filled with the Logos can discern meaning and a guiding purpose. The Aeon, however we interpret that word, is at one and

[1] Fragment 52 (in Diels, *Fragmente der Vorsokratiker,* 5th ed., I, p. 162, Berlin, 1934), preserved in Hippolytus, *Elenchus,* IX, 9, 4 (*GCS* III, p. 242, ll. 4–5). —For the interpretation cf. E. Zeller – W. Nestle, *Die Philosophie der Griechen,* 6th ed., I, 2, pp. 807–8, Leipzig, 1920.

[2] Friedrich Nietzsche, *Das Philosophenbuch,* I: "Die Philosophie im tragischen Zeitalter der Griechen" (Fragment Frühjahr 1873), No. 6, pp. 37ff., Leipzig, 1903.

[3] F. Lasalle, *Die Philosophie Herakleitos des Dunklen,* I, pp. 243f.—W. Nestle, "Heraklit und die Orphiker", in *Philologus,* 64 (1905), pp. 367–84.

[4] Fragment 125 (Diels, *Fragmente der Vorsokratiker,* I, p. 178).

the same time a king and a child, irresistible in his
almighty power, and yet light-hearted and free from
care as a child over his draught-board. His work is full
of meaning and in this sense royal, and yet it is un-
necessary and in that sense childish. It is all a divine game.
It is this dialectical paradox of king and child that
expresses the metaphysical nature of creation, and it is this
that makes it permissible for us to speak of a playing God.

So we find, not a closed cosmic system inexorably
obeying its own laws, but an order directed by the Logos
after the manner of a graceful game, a Logos who is
separate from the created world, not identical with it.
Heraclitus had grasped this truth, however dimly, and
those who subsequently worked out the Logos philosophy
were to make many references to the world order as a
divine game. Philo of Alexandria applies Heraclitus' idea
of the flux of all things to history in a grandiose survey of
political events. The justice of the great world plan is
ever striking new balances, creating and sweeping into
oblivion the great empires of men: Carthage, Greece,
Macedonia, all have come to nothing. As in a vigorous
world democracy, the various forces and tasks are continually being re-assigned. Yet there is nothing here of
the remorseless cruelty of an inexorable Tyche; it is all
the playing of the Logos. And here Philo uses the truly
remarkable words: "χορεύει γὰρ ἐν κύκλῳ λόγος ὁ θεῖος,
ὃν οἱ πολλοὶ τῶν ἀνθρώπων ὀνομάζουσι Τύχην – But the
divine Logos goes circling in his round, he whom many
men call Chance."[1] So this concept of the playing of God
makes transparent all the bright things of this world and
indeed all happenings, whatsoever their kind. "All

[1] Philo, *Quod Deus sit Immutabilis*, 172–6 (ed. Cohn–Wendland, II, p. 92,
ll. 5–23).

15

things are created by the life of the all in its fullness," says Plotinus, "and by living it creates gay multiplicity; it never ceases, but continues without pause to call into being lovely, well-formed, living playthings."[1] The visible is for these thinkers of the late Hellenic age—the culture that had grown so vividly aware of the transcendence of the divine—no more than an εἴδωλον – a phantom, "a children's tale", a παίγνιον θεοῦ, when set against true being. Visible things might be compared to the Athenian stories of Solon which—according to Plato[2]—were only children's fables of the "young" Athenians when set beside the age-old wisdom of the Egyptians. So says Proclus in his commentary on Plato's *Timaeus*.[3] "Others also say that he who fashioned the world was playing a game in his shaping of the cosmos, as Heraclitus already declared."[4]

The leading idea behind these philosophical speculations which conceived of the world's creation as a kind of game, had already found in the imagery of myths a more striking and direct expression—and perhaps one that penetrated even deeper towards the truth. In Heraclitus there still re-echoes the Orphic intimation of the dialectic which oscillates between world-creation and world-play, between king and child, and this thought is behind all the myths that tell of an infant god. Dionysus, Hermes, Apollo, Heracles were, in the first instance, all world-creating children, and K. Kerényi has shown[5] that the stories in question are not "biographical" myths at all, but mythical expressions of the divine nature, of the timeless being—

[1] Plotinus, *Enneads*, III, 2, 15 (ed. von Harder, V, p. 43).
[2] Plato, *Timaeus*, 23B.
[3] Proclus, *In Timaeum*, I, 39C (ed. Diehl, I, p. 127).
[4] Ibid., II, 101F (p. 334).
[5] Jung–Kerényi, *Essays on a Science of Mythology*, pp. 35ff. (by Kerényi).

at work even in the child—of him who is everlastingly
and irresistibly formative and creative, knowing all
things and doing all things, but as a child would know
and do them—in fact, of the God who brings forth everything, as it were, in play. Thus, in the Orphic fragment
which Clement of Alexandria has preserved, the infant
Dionysus plays with the bright playthings of which the
world is made up: "tops of different kinds and dolls with
moving limbs, apples too, the beautiful golden ones of
the clear-voiced daughters of Hesperus".[1]

Into the same group of myths we should certainly put
the toys of the child in the Theban myth of the Cabiri.[2]
It is a game with the world, a playing of the divine child
out of which worlds are created. We see the same thing
in the myth of the infant Zeus when his nurse Adrastea
fashions for him the sphere that is the beautiful ball of the
earth; it is with this that he plays in the cave on Mount
Ida.[3]

Apollonius Rhodius describes in the Third Book of his
Argonautica how Eros and Aphrodite play their fateful ball
game together, and Johann Jakob Bachofen has penetrated
deep into the meaning of all this divine ball play, though
he has perhaps gone too far in his generalizing: "In
Apollonius' account the ball thrown by Urania describes
a line of fire through the air like a star. In a fragment of
Sappho it is described as having a colour like that of
purple fire. These are flights of fancy, but they do still

---

[1] *Orphicorum Fragmenta*, 34 (ed. Kern, Berlin, 1922, pp. 110f.), quoted in
Clement of Alexandria, *Protrepticus*, II, 17, 2 (*GCS* I, p. 14, ll. 12–13).—
Cf. W. Willi in *Eranos-Jahrbuch*, 11 (1945), p. 76.

[2] Cf. O. Kern in *Realenzyklopädie* (ed. Pauly–Wissowa), 10 (1919),
col. 1440.

[3] Apollonius Rhodius, *Argonautica*, III, ll. 131 ff. [Engl. tr. in Penguin
Classics.]

convey clearly their primitive cosmic significance."[1]
Everywhere we find in such myths an intuitive feeling
that the world was not created under some kind of
constraint, that it did not unfold itself out of the divine in
obedience to some inexorable cosmic law; rather, it was
felt, was it born of a wise liberty, of the gay spontaneity of
God's mind; in a word, it came from the hand of a child.
"For the smile of the gods gave to the things of the cosmos
their being and their power to continue," says Proclus in
his commentary on the *Timaeus*,[2] and it is the infant
Logos who holds the sphere of the world within his
playing hands—the λόγος-παῖς or Logos-child. Yet, even
in Christian mysticism, that Logos-child is the symbol of
the tremendous tension between two apparent contradictories—between almighty power and childlike play,
between the strength of God and a child's weakness; we
can trace this symbolism from Valentine the Gnostic to
the "naked boy – the *nackichter Knabe*" of Meister Eck-
hardt. Here is the significance of those pictures of the
infant Jesus in mediaeval art that show him carrying the
sphere of the world in his hands—the "apple" in this
divinely light-hearted game with the cosmos. Similarly,
the *putti* of baroque art, playing like tiny giants with the
ball of the earth, are symbols in human form—symbols
whose meaning has perhaps already been partly lost—
of the nature of that original thought in the mind of God
that hurled forth the tremendous pyrotechnics of creation;
they are the last residual vestiges of the attempt to clothe
in visible form God's mighty playing with the world.
"In contrast to the children of men, these little brats have

[1] Johann Jakob Bachofen, *Urreligion und Symbole* (ed. C. A. Bernoulli),
pp. 476–7, Leipzig, 1926.
[2] Proclus, *In Timaeum*, III, 147D (ed. Diehl, II, p. 27, l. 26); cf. ibid.,
III, 169C (p. 98, ll. 12–14).

the world behind them and around them, from heaven to hell . . . they are everlasting children, no dwarfs, rather arrested giants."[1]

Almost without noticing it we have come close to certain ideas which did not originate solely in the ponderings of philosophers or in mythical intimations; we are in contact with ideas that came from the word of revelation in Holy Scripture itself. Of the Divine Wisdom (*Ḥochmah*) we are told that from the beginning of time it had been playing before the face of the world-creating God. Thanks to that image the tentative perceptions the Greek Fathers had gained from Plato and Plotinus were, under the power of the word of God, formed into their admirable theology of the God that played. The text from Proverbs (8. 27–31) runs as follows:

When he established the heavens, I was there, . . .
when he marked out the foundations of the earth,
then I was beside him, like a little child;
and I was daily his delight,
rejoicing before him always,
rejoicing in his inhabited world
and delighting in the sons of men.

Here, in a poetic dramatization, the Wisdom of God is regarded as an hypostasis,[2] which is "with God" and on which the Creator of the world casts his delighted eye, as he brings visible things into being. "Hochmah was with God in the way that the ideal form is ever present to

---

[1] R. Gläser, *Ein himmlischer Kindergarten*. Munich, 1939. (Quoted from Jung–Kerényi, *Einführung in das Wesen der Mythologie*, German edition, p. 8.)

[2] P. Heinisch, *Personifikationen und Hypostasen im Alten Testament und im Alten Orient*, pp. 29–30. Münster, 1921—J. Göttsberger, *Die göttliche Weisheit als Persönlichkeit im Alten Testament*, pp. 28–9. Münster, 1919.

the artist as the dynamic agent in his creative work."[1]
But wisdom is the "little child" of God—though there is
some doubt whether this expression conveys the meaning
of the original word which only occurs in this one context.
This Wisdom "makes play before him", or rather, to be
more exact, "before his face"; it plays like a carefree
child, and in its movements the Creator of the world
beholds the loveliness of the world he is to fashion. We
can probably read a deeper meaning into this mysterious
phrase about *Hochmah* at play if we examine the actual
Hebrew wording used in this passage.[2] The word in
question occurs in two other passages of the Old Testament,
namely in II Kings [Samuel] 6. 5 and 21. Here it
definitely means to dance. In the first of these two
passages we read—or should read: "David and the
house of Israel danced before the Lord with all their
heart." Similarly when David is defending himself before
his wife Michal, he exclaims: "Before the Lord, yea,
before the Lord, will I dance!" The Septuagint has the
verb παίζοντες in both places, and the second time
strengthens it by saying: "παίζομαι καὶ ὀρχήσομαι – I
will play and dance." Let us, therefore, take the glorious
passage in Proverbs as: "I was daily his delight; I danced
before him always; I danced upon his round earth."
Whether that rendering be exact or not,[3] we certainly
come very close to the meaning of this word if we speak
of the dancing and playing of Divine Wisdom, of the
child's games when the world was made.

[1] A. Hudal, *Die religiösen und sittlichen Ideen des Spruchbuches*, p. 150,
Rome, 1914.

[2] I owe this suggestion to Mr R. Stecher of Innsbruck.

[3] [None of the various modern versions consulted does, in fact, use the
verb "dance" or an equivalent consistently in all the passages mentioned.
—*Translator*.]

Unfortunately the problem which this text presented to the exegete was made more intractable throughout the ages by the fact that in the case of Proverbs 8. 30 and 31, the Septuagint speaks neither of playing nor of dancing but of rejoicing [as in the text of the RSV given above], and the words read by the Greek Fathers in verse 31 are in fact: "ὅτε εὐφραίνετο τὴν οἰκουμένην συντελέσας – when he was rejoicing after completing his work on the earth." The old Latin version reads similarly, at any rate it also speaks of "rejoicing": "*Iucundabar ante faciem eius in omni tempore, cum laetaretur orbe perfecto* – I was gay before his face all the time when he was rejoicing over the completing of the earth."[1] Thus the idea of the Divine Wisdom's playing—or dancing—was one with which the Greek and Latin Fathers were no longer familiar. Even so, the picture of God rejoicing over the completion of the world still has about it something of the delight taken by the artist in his own free-roving fancy and so keeps alive the idea of play.

We must, however, also note that in the Greek version the word translated above as "little child", the word, it must be remembered, that only occurs in this one text —where it is applied to the Divine Wisdom—is paraphrased as "παρ᾽ αὐτῷ ὁρμόζουσα – creating alongside him and in harmony with him", the harmony that, as it were, accompanies God in his work of creation. This finds an echo in the tradition of the earliest Latin Fathers. In Tertullian, for instance, the Divine Wisdom is spoken of as "*modulans cum ipso* – ordering, regulating together with him"; and again as "*compingens cum ipso*" which one might render as "composing, fixing, adjusting the world

[1] Petrus Sabatier, *Bibliorum Sacrorum Latinae Versiones Antiquae*, II, p. 311, Paris, 1751.

with him".[1] And so the "play" or "dance" which the Creator of the world regards with such delight is the fullness of creative thought mirrored in Wisdom, in the Logos. "That is, the Wisdom in which God was rejoicing all the time", so runs Origen's interpretation of Proverbs, "when the earth had been made complete; and from this we are to understand that God is always full of joy. In this Wisdom that was always with the Father there is everlastingly foreshadowed and prefigured creation, and there never was a time when Wisdom did not contain such a prefigurement (*praefiguratio*) of that which was to come."[2]

Thanks to Jerome's improved translation it became generally known from the fourth century onwards that it was expressly of the "playing" of Divine Wisdom that the Scriptures were speaking here, but the interpretation of the cryptic passage was strongly affected by a desire to leave no loophole in it for the Arian doctrine, which denied that the Logos and the Father were of the same nature. "Did Wisdom, that is, the Son of God, indeed play before the face of the Father like a child?" asks Salonius in his mystical commentary on the wisdom literature, and his answer is: "By no means. When it is said that he played, this must be understood as meaning that he rejoiced, and the words 'He played before him all the days' mean that he rejoiced to be one with the Father, to be of one substance with him from the begin-

---

[1] Tertullian, *Adversus Hermogenem*, 18, 4 (*PL* 2, 236c ff.; *CC* 1, p. 412, ll. 24ff.); 32, 2 (*PL* 2, 251B; *CC* 1, p. 424, ll. 7ff.). [Engl. tr. in *ACW*, 24.] Cf. Irenaeus, *Adversus Haereses*, IV, 20, 3 (*PG* 7, 1034A); Cyprian, *Testimonia*, II, 1 (*CSEL* 3, 1, p. 62, ll. 12–14); Hilary, *In Psalmos*, 135, 13 (*PL* 9, 775B).

[2] Origen, *De Principiis*, I, 4, 4 (*GCS* V, p. 67, ll. 10–15).—Cf. Idem, *In Ioannem*, I, 9 (*GCS* IV, p. 14, ll. 26–30); Clement Al., *Stromata*, VII, 2, 7, 4 (*GCS* III, p. 7, ll. 10–11).

ning, before all the days of eternity. But how did he play upon the earth always? Because even when the time came for the earth to be made and for creatures to come into being, he rejoiced that for all time, remaining in the Father, he was that which he was and is."[1] Here then the mystical play of the Logos finds a place in the innermost being of the Triune God. If we look at the matter from this point of view, we begin to understand why the delight of the Father in his Son could overflow on to the earth and all its varied beauty which had been prefigured in the Eternal Wisdom.

I have still to quote one more commentator who wrote at the beginning of our own time and was possessed of a remarkably perceptive sense for things of this kind. He remarks of the divine child's play: "The Son is called a child because of his proceeding everlastingly from the Father, because in the dewy freshness and spring-time beauty of his eternal youth he eternally enacts a game before his Father."[2]

Some lines from a poem by Gregory Nazianzen, which later Greek theologians were never to forget, show how very much alive this mystical idea of the playing of the world Logos remained among the Greek Fathers of the Church—despite the infelicitous translation and its effects in the handing down of the text from Proverbs:

παίζει γὰρ λόγος αἰπύς, ἐν εἴδεσι παντοδαποῖσι
κίρνας, ὡς ἐθέλει, κόσμον ὅλον ἔνθα καὶ ἔνθα.[3]

(For the Logos on high plays,
stirring the whole cosmos back and forth, as he wills,
into shapes of every kind.)

[1] Salonius, *Expositio Mystica in Parabolas Salomonis* (*PL* 53, 974AB).— Later in the same sense: Bede, *Super Parabolas Salomonis Allegorica Expositio*, I, 8 (*PL* 91, 966B); Hrabanus Maurus, *Expositio in Proverbia Salomonis*, I, 8 (*PL* 111, 710A); *Glossa Ordinaria in Proverbia*, 8. 31 (*PL* 113, 1091D).

[2] Cornelius a Lapide, *Commentaria in Proverbia*, 8. 31, Nota tertio, Mystice.

[3] Gregory Nazianzen, *Carmina*, I, 2, 2, vv. 589–90 (*PG* 37, 624A f.).

No less a man than Maximus Confessor, whose closely related turn of mind made of him the perfect elucidator of the more obscure phases of Gregory's thought, was moved by these verses to work out an entire mystical theology of this playing of God,[1] and here, at what is perhaps the very highest level of Greek theological speculation on this subject, we are once more made to see just what it is that this imagery was seeking to convey. It is that both creation and incarnation are expressions of God's love, and that this love, though full of meaning and purpose, is a love that works in creative freedom wholly ungoverned by necessity or constraint, but that in view of the very superabundance of the divine φρόνησις we can only speak of such immense things in terms of a purely negative theology—as Paul spoke of the foolishness and weakness of God. It is in this spirit and under this constraint that we speak of the playing of God, who through this creative pouring out of himself makes it possible for the creature to understand him in the wonderful play of his works; who has made for us children's toys out of the bright and variegated forms of his world wherewith to educate us, his true παίγνια, for things unseen and eternal things which are real and earnest. The whole game of the Logos which he enacts upon the earth to the delight of the Father, his cosmic dance on the globe of the world, is only a playful hint of what has reposed since before the beginning of time in the divine archetypes of Eternal Wisdom, and of what will be revealed when the earthly dance has come to an end. "For this earthly life," says Maximus in reference to Gregory's poem, "compared with the life to come, the true, divine,

---

[1] Maximus, *Ambigua*, 261a (*PG* 91, 1408ff.).

archetypal life (πρὸς τὴν μέλλουσαν τῆς θείας καὶ ἀληθοῦς ζωῆς ἀρχετυπίαν), is but a children's game.[1]

We see here how Plato's concept of man as the πταίγνιον of the God who plays has found a place in a Christian and mystical philosophy of life, and from this point it is now possible to proceed to a deeper conception of the playing of man. This I am going to try to elaborate in the second part of this enquiry, for, since God is a *Deus vere ludens*, man too must be a creature that plays: a *Homo ludens*.

In his thoughtful commentary on the cosmic theology of Maximus[2] Hans Urs von Balthasar has admirably summarized the matter: "Once this exalted viewpoint has been attained," he writes, "all the dissonances of this world are, for Maximus as for any other, resolved in a final harmony. 'Whatever possesses existence is formed in accordance with a perfect law and is incapable of having part in a better one.'[3] Whoever seeks to grasp and describe this harmony must possess in his pursuit of knowledge that easy and relaxed lightness of heart which finds expression in the peace of this vision. Whoever has, even for a moment, caught sight of this vast cosmic game will thenceforward at all times know that the little life of man and all the seriousness thereof is only a vanishing figure in this dance. 'We ourselves,' says Maximus, 'begotten and born like the other beasts, we who then become children and move forward from youth to the wrinkles of old age, we who are like flowers which last but for a moment and who then die and are transported into that other life—truly we deserve to be looked upon as a children's game played by God.' "[4]

[1] Ibid., 263a (*PG* 91, 1416c).
[2] Hans Urs von Balthasar, *Kosmische Liturgie*. Maximus der Bekenner, Höhe und Krise des griechischen Weltbildes, pp. 7–8, Freiburg, 1941.
[3] Maximus, *Ambigua* (*PG* 91, 1189D).   [4] Ibid., 263a (*PG* 91, 1416c).

II

The Playing of Man

Man, according to Plotinus, is a "living plaything", though he is more than a mere token which can be moved or thrown away in play as an unpredictable mood may dictate. He is prefigured in the Logos, the object of a divine artist's joy, and so, as we have already seen— and as Plato tells us, the best thing about him is that he himself should be a player—one who, in all the multiplicity of activities that proceed out of the nature of his created being, imitates, as far as in him lies, the quality of God's own creative power by his lightness of touch, by his regard for beauty, by his wisdom and by the sober seriousness of his endeavour. This eager lightness of touch is never mere frivolity, for frivolity is always the sign of a secret despair; whereas he who plays this game of God is secure in the knowledge that he proceeds unceasingly from God's own creating and protecting hand. The man who plays after this fashion is one who is in earnest about life, because he knows two things and holds them both together: he knows that his life has meaning and that his existence in creation is not the product of necessity.

Now these two pieces of knowledge reveal two aspects of our earthly life of which the man who truly plays will never cease to be keenly aware. The first is that existence is a joyful thing, because it is secure in God; the second, that it is also a tragic thing, because freedom must always

26

involve peril. It is, as Plato says in the *Philebus*, a mixture of joy and sorrow, a comedy and a tragedy in one;[1] for there is no play that has not something profoundly serious at the bottom of it, and even when children play, they come, with all the compulsion of characters in a myth, under the spell of absolute obligation and under the shadow of the possibility that the game may be lost.

From this dialectical tension, which cannot be resolved as long as we are spirits clothed in matter, there arises one characteristic of man at play which I select for discussion from a whole host of others: he who plays after this fashion is the "grave-merry" man, once again in that untranslatable Greek phrase, the ἀνὴρ σπουδογέλοιος. I am trying to make plain that such a man is really always two men in one: he is a man with an easy gaiety of spirit, one might almost say a man of spiritual elegance, a man who feels himself to be living in invincible security; but he is also a man of tragedy, a man of laughter and tears, a man, indeed, of gentle irony, for he sees through the tragically ridiculous masks of the game of life and has taken the measure of the cramping boundaries of our earthly existence.

And so, only one who can fuse these two contradictory elements into a spiritual unity is indeed a man who truly plays. If he is only the first of these two things, we must write him down as a frivolous person who has, precisely, played himself out. If he is only the second, then we must account him as one who cannot conquer despair. It is the synthesis of the two things that makes the *Homo ludens*, the "grave-merry" man, the man with a gentle sense of humour who laughs despite his tears, and finds in all earthly mirth a sediment of insufficiency. This

[1] Plato, *Philebus*, 50B.

grave-merriness—the wonderful word "humour" has been worn so threadbare, has indeed been so grossly misused— is something suspended between heaven and earth. "Humour cannot be thought of save in a temporal setting," writes Theodor Haecker in his *Tag- und Nacht-bücher*; "yet it is also one of those things that are unthinkable without eternity,"[1] and he wrote this in the midst of the horror of the German *débâcle* when the only acknowledged value was the grimy, unrelieved earnestness of a devilish utilitarianism.

My meaning now will be reasonably plain. I see the real inwardness of this great synthesis of which I speak in a kind of Mozartian suspension between laughter and tears, between merriment and patience, a state of the soul in which the early Fathers of the Church wrote some of their loveliest pages, speaking of this our earthly life as a "divine children's game".

The man who truly plays is, therefore, first of all, a man in whom seriousness and gaiety are mingled; and, indeed, at the bottom of all play there lies a tremendous secret. We had some intimation of it, surely, when we were considering the creative play of God. All play—just as much as every task which we set ourselves to master with real earnestness of purpose—is an attempt to approximate to the Creator, who performs his work with the divine seriousness which its meaning and purpose demand, and yet with the spontaneity and effortless skill of the great artist he is, creating because he wills to create and not because he must.

Plotinus had an inkling of this when he wrote that all things, including play, strive towards θεωρία, towards the vision of God in which we are made like him. Plotinus

[1] Theodor Haecker, *Tag- und Nachtbücher*, p. 285, Olten, 1948.

actually begins this treatise with something of the grace and elegance of a good player playing a game: "Making play to begin with before taking up the subject seriously, we affirm: All things strive towards *theoria*, the vision of God. Does that mean that this treatise of mine is itself nothing but a kind of game? For, after all, things that play, play only because of their urge to attain to the vision of God, whether they are the seriousness of the grown man, or the play of the child."[1]

Now, why is this so? Is it not because mere seriousness does not get down to the roots of things, and because a spirit of fun, of irony and of humour often digs deeper and seems to get more easily—because more playfully—down to the truth? Surely Xenophon had caught sight of at least a part of this truth when he begins his *Symposium* thus: "I hold the view that the works of good and lovable men are worthy of memory, not only when they have been carried out in a serious vein (μετὰ σπουδῆς) but also when this has been done in a spirit of play (ἐν ταῖς παιδιαῖς)."[2] Plato in the *Laws* voices a similar sentiment when he says that the truly temperate man (τελέως σώφρων ἀνήρ) must prove himself to be such in his play as much as in his serious work.[3] This happy mingling of the light-hearted and the serious is a flower that grows only midway betwixt heaven and earth—in the man who loves this bright and colourful world and yet can smile at it, who knows in his heart that it has proceeded from God but also knows its limits. Within those limits, and because of them, things knock into each other, thus producing comedy—but also tragedy. These may annoy us; we can

[1] Plotinus, *Enneads*, III, 8, 1 (ed. Harder, III, p. 1).
[2] Xenophon, *Symposium/Convivium*, I, 1.
[3] Plato, *Laws*, 647D.

react angrily or we can accept them with calm good humour. They can disconcert us and still, at the same time, delight us in our vision directed always towards the Logos in his "co-fashioning" action, for it is in him that everything has its source and it is towards the vision of him that all our play ultimately tends. Without the divine drop of oil we call humour the great world machine would soon grind to a standstill.

The wise men among the Greeks, those true *ludimagistri*, knew all this even better than we do today. Ludwig Radermacher, the master whose own wisdom came from that source, has made that clear in his book on tears and laughter and I am indebted to him because of the stimulus he gave me.[1] For Xenophon παίζειν σπουδῇ, the ability to play while preserving a serious frame of mind, is accounted as a thing of high value in the art of fashioning life.[2] Strabo calls the comic dramatist Menippus a σπουδογέλοιος,[3] and Diogenes Laertius extols Heraclitus, the poet and philosopher, using the same term.[4] To them, the art, superhuman in its difficulty, of a spiritual culture that is truly humane, appeared—and rightly—to reside in the ability to take life seriously and yet be able to play and while playing ever to keep a serious corner in one's mind. To keep an open heart for the things of this world and never to fly from the world through contempt for them, and yet always to remain detached from them, knowing that they must not be taken too seriously. "This was the way in which Socrates jested about these things, though with serious intent

---

[1] Ludwig Radermacher, *Weinen und Lachen*. Studien über antikes Lebensgefühl, Vienna, 1947.

[2] Xenophon, *Cyropaedia*, VI, 1, 6; VIII, 3, 47.

[3] Strabo, *Geography*, XVI, 29.

[4] Diogenes Laertius, *Vitae et Placita Philosophorum*, IX, 1, 17.

– ἔπαιζεν ἄμα σπουδάζων," says Xenophon at the end of one of the thoughtful works this gay master wrote.[1]

It seems hardly necessary for me to point to the depth of feeling and thought that so often marks the jesting and clowning of Aristophanes, or, for that matter, to the humour of Shakespeare in which every phase and aspect of life is so gloriously revealed. Yet I must quote the choral ode in the *Frogs* that is addressed to Demeter, the queen of the pure orgies. In this there is a hint that the jesting of comedy is in the last resort a kind of dance around the truth:

> Let me never cease throughout the day
> to play, to dance, to sing.
> Let me utter many a quip,
> let me also say much meant in earnest.
> And if my playing and mockery be worthy of thy feast,
> let me be crowned with the garland of victory.[2]

Lucian, the satirist, was another who understood that in the Greek theatre there was more wisdom concealed behind the humour—and revealed—than the outward slickness of mimicry and gesture might lead one to suppose. "I have always returned from the theatre a wiser man," he writes to his earnest and rather simple-minded opponent in his work on the dance, "and with a rather better knowledge of life."[3] And here there comes into his mind a line of Homer's with which I have already dealt extensively elsewhere.[4] It is the passage where the

[1] Xenophon, *Memorabilia*, I, 3, 8.
[2] Aristophanes, *Frogs*, vv. 387ff.
[3] Lucian, *De Saltatione*, 4 (Jacobitz [Bibliotheca Teubneriana], II, p. 145).
[4] Hugo Rahner, *Greek Myths and Christian Mystery*, pp. 329ff., London, 1963.

Sirens promise Odysseus, as he sails past, a more profound knowledge that would be given him in the midst of pleasure. The returning seafarer, the Sirens say, will "sail away full of joy and with new knowledge – τερψάμενος νεῖται καὶ πλείονα εἰδώς".[1]

Whether or no the Sirens' promise is really a legitimate illustration of the point, the truth seized upon by Lucian remains, and the irresolvable dialectic of this "joyful philosophy" resides in the fact that the deeper levels of serious knowledge cannot be plumbed without some admixture of the opposite qualities of gaiety and even a taste for the ridiculous. Plato had already been teaching that to the world: "Without some recognition of the ridiculous, it is impossible to understand properly the serious aspect of things, as, in general, when we are dealing with contradictories, one factor in the contradiction cannot be understood without the other."[2] In a word, all that appertains to play is only a rehearsal for what is serious. Aristotle teaches the same lesson, even though, compared with Plato, he tends somewhat to narrow its application.[3] In the same way, Huizinga's *Homo Ludens* is really more concerned with serious matters than with play.

We can perceive this truth from yet a different angle. Any man who can truly see the transcendental relation of all created things to God will avoid applying to the consideration of even the most serious things a seriousness that wholly distorts them. He knows—and wisely recognizes the fact with a wry smile—that even the greatest deeds of men are but children's games compared with the perfection which our souls desire or the perfection that is

---

[1] Homer, *Odyssey*, XII, 188.   [2] Plato, *Laws*, 816DE.
[3] Aristotle, *Politics*, 1337B.—Plato, *Laws*, 643C; 794A.

in God himself. Indeed, in all his thinking, his pondering, his fashioning and designing, he is but a poor imitator of the Logos, the Heavenly Wisdom who plays upon the earth, the co-fashioner with God.

Plato once called the *Phaedrus*, one of the most profound of his dialogues, a παίγνιον – a plaything; he did so, because, in Radermacher's words, "in his eyes which saw so far beyond the busy preoccupations of men, jest and earnest lay very close to each other and were not always readily distinguishable".[1] In much the same spirit Plato refers in the *Laws* to the extremely serious political activity of the wise old men of Athens as "an intelligent children's game (παιδιὰ λολική) played by old men",[2] as though it were a kind of indefatigable tinkering with the problem of the greatest possible public good, an activity not unlike that of the artist who is never completely satisfied with his work and who "as one in play" must ever be starting and experimenting anew. That is why the seven wise men in Plutarch's *Symposium* laugh as they pronounce the truths they have to declare; and if one of the very greatest but perhaps all too serious classical scholars of our day, namely U. von Wilamowitz, considers this work no more than a rather clumsy kind of joke,[3] we may surely quote against him the jesting wisdom of Radermacher: "These", writes the latter, "are the sentiments of a man whose soul is at home upon the lofty heights of Pindar, Aeschylus and Plato. There is a pathos to which laughter is alien and even repulsive. Yet may it not perhaps be possible to surmount such pathos by a philosophy that conceives of life in terms of contra-

---

[1] Radermacher, *op. cit.*, p. 96.
[2] Plato, *Laws*, 796A.
[3] Thus U. von Wilamowitz, *Hermes*, 25, p. 196 note.

dictions and can make a man a master of the serious by means of its opposite?"[1]

There is a fine essay by E. R. Curtius in which he speaks of this truly humanist ideal of the "grave-merry" man.[2] He refers to a passage from the letters of the younger Pliny, a passage which is eloquent of the inward balance of a wise man of the good Roman kind. It is an attitude of Stoic acquiescence in things as they are, but one which leaves the mind open to the hidden things of a higher order. "As in my life, so in my studies I consider it most fitting for a true man (*humanissimum*) to mingle a mild and cheerful spirit (*comitas*) with my more serious mood, so that seriousness should not fall away into mere melancholy nor jest into mere licence. Guided by this principle, I now and then interrupt my more serious work with jollity and play."[3] Aelius Spartianus' description of the Emperor Hadrian's character is another example. I quote it because, in its dialectical pregnancy, it is a perfect illustration of the spiritual attitude that I have designated by the words *Homo ludens*, for that unfettered attainment of the happy mean that marks the "grave-merry" man. The Emperor is spoken of as "*severus comis, gravis lascivus, simulator simplex, et semper in omnibus varius* – stern and friendly, serious and wanton, cunning and simple and in all things a mixture of various elements".[4]

It is at this point that we should be beginning to understand the peril which such an attitude involves; for only the man who knows just where to find the middle region between heaven and earth will, with sure instinct, fall into this balanced posture of the soul that is the mark

[1] Radermacher, *op. cit.*, p. 78.
[2] E. R. Curtius, *Romanische Forschungen*, 53 (1939), pp. 1ff.
[3] Pliny the Younger, *Epistulae*, VIII, 21, 1.
[4] Aelius Spartianus, *Vita Hadriani*, XIV, 11.

of the man who plays rightly. He must be a man who neither cynically despises the world nor is consumed by an epicurean appetite for it; he must be a man who has the divine so much at the centre of his preoccupations that he can find it in the things of this world. In other words, the nature of the inward gaiety of the man who truly plays, and for whom earnest and jest are sisters, is at bottom a religious problem, and this peculiar quality can only be attained by one who is both of heaven and of earth. Kierkegaard has written words which make this plain for all time,[1] and a philosopher who has been touched by his spirit has recently written the following: "The inner essence of humour lies, no matter how heretical this may seem, in the strength of the religious disposition; for what humour does is to note how far all earthly and human things fall short of the measure of God."[2] Theodor Haecker is, therefore, most certainly right when he declares that this thing we call humour constitutes the real human background of the civilization of European Christendom.[3]

This then seems to be the place where I may usefully add a few words on the ideal of the "grave-merry" man as a Christian will tend to interpret it; for it is surely clear that it is only through our faith in the Incarnation, our faith in God's truly having become man, that it is made possible for us to gain that "gay security and freedom" without which we cannot attain the ease and effortlessness of genuine play at all.

[1] Sören Kierkegaard, *Concluding Unscientific Postscript.* Tr. by David F. Swenson and Walter Lowrie, pp. 400–4; 451–68, London, 1941.

[2] P. Lersch, *Die Philosophie des Humors,* quoted in E. Ortmann, "Humor und Erziehung: Situation und Entscheidung", in *Zeitbuch für Politik und Kultur,* I, p. 163, Warendorf, 1947.—Cf. also H. S. Braun, *Vom Humor des Christen. Ein Kapitel über frohe und unfrohe Frömmigkeit,* Paderborn, 1940.

[3] Theodor Haecker, *Wiederbegegnungen von Kirche und Kultur in Deutschland,* p. 165.

And that brings me to the Christian saints. What were they after all but men who enacted for our benefit a children's game played before God, a game from which every vestige of the tragic has completely disappeared. This applies as much to the Egyptian Fathers of the Thebaid, so stern and grim in their outward semblance, as to a man of such palpable and engaging charm as St Francis de Sales who made the famous remark: "A sad saint is a sorry sort of saint!"

In the essay by Curtius to which I have already alluded and which appeared under the title *Die Kirche und das Lachen* – "The Church and Laughter", the author has gathered together a quantity of material which illustrates the nature of this ideal of the "grave-merry" man in its Christian transfiguration. One sees from it how easily gaiety came to the Christian. An excellent example is the seventy-third chapter of Athanasius' famous life of St Anthony where he speaks of the well-nigh heavenly gaiety of this father of asceticism: "τὸν δὲ λόγον εἶχεν ἠρτυμένον τῷ θείῳ ἅλατι – his speech was seasoned with divine salt."[1] Sulpicius Severus says much the same of that father of Western monasticism, St Martin of Tours. He tells us some of the jests of the saint, saying that they were *"spiritualiter salsa* – spiritually salted".[2]

This Christian ideal of the "grave-merry" man born as it was out of classical humanism and the Christian sense of redemption was long to remain alive. Hugh of St Victor declared that serious things tasted better if spiced with kindly mockery,[3] and John of Salisbury

---

[1] Athanasius, *Vita Antonii*, 73 (*PG* 26, 945A). [Engl. tr. in *ACW*, 10.]— On the Desert Fathers and their lack of humour, cf. K. Heussi, *Der Ursprung des Mönchtums*, pp. 246ff., Tübingen, Mohr, 1936.

[2] Sulpicius Severus, *Dialogi*, II, 10 (*CSEL* 1, p. 191).

[3] Quoted in Curtius, *Romanische Forschungen*, 53 (1939), p. 8.

wrote in his *Polycraticus*: "It is a pleasant thing and in no way contrary to a good man's honour that he should here and there unbend and be moved by seemly mirth (*modesta hilaritate*)."[1] Or again we have those neat lines by Hildebert of Le Mans:

Admittenda tibi ioca sunt post seria quaedam,
   sed tamen et dignis ipsa gerenda modis.[2]

(Permit thyself a few jests in the midst of thy serious work, but even thy jesting should be carried out in a worthy manner.)

A smile is itself a sign of wisdom—so thought the Greek Fathers.[3] Indeed Origen, exaggerating the easy and relaxed quality of mind that should always mark the Christian, goes so far as to say that the truly wise man is like a child that smiles and plays by the bier of its parents.[4] A mediaeval theologian poses the question whether Christ ever laughed, for he was truly man and to be able to laugh is part of our human nature.[5] And so, I maintain, among the truly great Christians there have always been *ioculatores Domini*, even greater than the *ioculator Basiliensis* of Hesse's *Glasperlenspiel*, for the simple reason that they have been both greater lovers of the world and also more detached from it.

This gaiety in play however has another side to it. Man, in spite of his play, will always return to that gentle melancholy which we can already feel in Plato, though

---

[1] John of Salisbury, *Polycraticus*, I, 8 (*PL* 199, 406B).
[2] Hildebert of Le Mans, *Libellus de IV Virtutibus Vitae Honestae* (*PL* 171, 1060C).
[3] Methodius of Philippi, *De Lepra*, 13, 5 (*GCS*, p. 468, ll. 9–15).
[4] Origen, *In Matthaeum*, 13, 16 (*GCS* X, p. 220, ll. 20–3).—Cf. W. Völker, *Das Vollkommenheitsideal des Origenes*, p. 55, Tübingen, Mohr, 1931.
[5] Petrus Cantor, *Verbum Abbreviatum*, 67 (*PL* 205, 203CD).

in a manner and degree dependent both on his general spiritual make-up and on his personal experience of life; for life itself is a game that can often play us nasty tricks, and we tend to think it contrary to our spiritual nature and unworthy of it that, being enmeshed as we are in the earthly and material, we should be exposed to the seemingly malignant buffets of chance. The more a truly spiritual man feels that God alone "is worthy of being taken with blessed seriousness"—to quote Plato once again—the more he must feel that he has been caught up in a kind of play here below which he must carry on with dignity—for the role of our earthly life must be played through to the end—but which we must recognize for what it is; never for a moment must we lose sight of the unreal and transitory quality of the scenery and stage properties that surround us.

Plotinus has expressed all this in one of the most moving passages in his whole work on the mysticism of play. In it he treats all earthly matters, be they politics, conquests, murder, sudden death or any of the other constituents of what we call history, as forming a single great theatrical performance: "All this is no more than so many changes of scene and shiftings of properties, so many simulated tears and rehearsed lamentations." He, however, who has no foundation in the divine confuses such play-acting with reality—or falls into a mimic despair.

Here no doubt there speaks the unbridled "spiritualism" of the Neoplatonist, but we can also detect the voice of a profound experience, a knowledge of life that has acquired a certain melancholy tint: "It is not the soul but only the outer shadow of a man that enacts this play. He who only knows how to live in the nether world of externals never understands that, however real his tears may appear to himself, he is only acting a part; for it is only with the most serious and noble part of ourselves that we must seriously concern ourselves with serious things. All else about us is vanity and make-believe. Yet those who do not really know what it means to be serious are just the men who take everything seriously in their play, for they are nothing but vain playthings themselves. Socrates may have played at times—but only with the outward Socrates.[1]

It is plain enough from these words that the *homo vere ludens* is a man who reserves all that is serious in him for the things of the next world, and because about those things he is very serious indeed, he can never be a man who wholly loses himself in play. Neither can he be a man who despairs.

For these two fates are really the same and none knew this better than Hölderlin when he cried out to the poets who had lost themselves in a kind of idyll of playfulness: "Must you be for ever playing and jesting? You cannot help it! O friends, this strikes me to the heart, for this is the compulsion of despair."[2] But the man who is at the exact midpoint between heaven and earth, the Christian, the true gnostic, can conceive of his life and of all the happenings in the world as something best described by the apt metaphor of Plotinus: a single great theatrical performance, for he knows something of the secrets of what is behind the stage. That is why he can do so without agonizing over the state of the world or greedily desiring the things it has to offer. For him earnest and jest are indeed sisters in God. And so the true gnostic "faultlessly plays to the end the part in the drama of life for which God

[1] Plotinus, *Enneads*, III, 2, 15 (ed. Harder, V, p. 44).
[2] *Hölderlins sämtliche Werke* (ed. by F. Seebass), IV, p. 3, Berlin, 1923.

has cast him," says Clement of Alexandria, "for he knows
what he must do and what he must bear"[1]—a piece
of Stoic wisdom irradiated by Christian light! In that
philosophy the great world masterpieces of the stage
have their roots, from Calderón to Hofmannsthal. How
admirably, for instance, is it expressed in Fortunio's lines
in Hofmannsthal's *Der weisse Fächer – The White Fan*:

> I know but little, yet have I cast a glance
> Into the depths and this have recognized:
> This life is nothing more than shadow-play.
> So, lightly let your eyes glance over it;
> Then you can bear it. Yet if you hold it fast
> It crumbles in your fingers.[2]

Surely only a man whose foundation is in the reality of
God can thus call life on earth a game and a shadow-
play? For only to such a man as this, only to a man who
truly believes that this world has proceeded out of the
fullness of God's creative being, is it given to say "Nay"
along with his "Yea", and to say it without demur or
hesitation. In other words, only such a man can accept
and lovingly embrace the world—which includes himself
—as God's handiwork, and, at the same time, toss it
aside as a child would toss a toy of which it had wearied,
in order then to soar upward into the "blessed seriousness" which is God alone. Only thus does gay melancholy become both possible and justified, the mood
which must always govern the Christian, the true *Homo
ludens*, as he follows his middle road. Love for the world
and rejection of the world—both of these must draw

[1] Clement Al., *Stromata*, VII, 11, 65, 6 (*GCS* III, p. 47, ll. 7–9).
[2] Hugo von Hofmannsthal, *Der weisse Fächer*, ein Zwischenspiel, Leipzig.
1907.

him and he must at one and the same moment be ready to fold that world in his embrace and to turn his back upon it.

In a few words full of inimitable Greek dialectic, Maximus (who commented on Gregory's verses about the playing Logos) puts what is basically the same truth in rather a different form. The transitory life of man is a game, because it is an "ἐπίρρυπος καὶ εὐαλλοίωτος στάσις – a stable state that is ever subject to flux and capable of continual change", or contrariwise, "a flow that is for ever becoming static – στάσιμος ῥεῦσις".[1] The thought was inspired by Gregory's wonderful funeral oration on Caesarius: "The life of man, my brethren, is but a fleeting moment of being alive; it is a children's game played upon the earth . . . a shadow you cannot hold, the flight of a passing bird, a ship on the sea leaving no wake, dust, mist, morning dew and a bursting blossom."[2] Indeed so familiar was this concept of life as a theatrical performance, no doubt, though one with a hidden meaning that would one day be made plain, that Augustine could speak of life's being a farce without any fear of being misunderstood. The children whom the parents had longed to have, he tells his flock, are just those who are all too anxious to get their parents off the stage so that they can do a bit of play-acting themselves. They come and cry: " '*Eia, cogitate ire hinc, agamus et nos mimum nostrum* – Hey! It really is time for you to be off. We want to act our little play.' This life of ours is a comedy, imperilled as it is. For it is written: 'Naught but vanity is every man living' (Ps. 38. 6)."[3]

---

[1] Maximus, *Ambigua*, 262b (*PG* 91, 1412B).
[2] Gregory Nazianzen, *Orationes*, VII, 19 (*PG* 35, 777CD).
[3] Augustine, *Enarrationes in Psalmos*, 127, 15 (*PL* 36, 1686).

41

Life then, as has already been said, has this dual character. It is gay because secure in God, it is tragic because our freedom continually imperils it, and so the man who truly plays must be both gay and serious at the same time; we must find him both smiling and in tears. His portion, if I may here bring in the profound synthesis of the Fathers, will be both joy and perseverance.

There is an allegory that I want to rescue from oblivion, for it is indeed a pearl of great price. It clothes with its wonderful imagery the very real understanding which the Christians of antiquity possessed of the nature of this children's game our life is. The allegory is built up on a text in Genesis (26. 8) in which we are told how Isaac and his wife Rebecca went during a time of famine into the land of the Philistines to King Abimelech. In order to safeguard his life, Isaac gave out that Rebecca was his sister, but one day the king looking out through a window saw Isaac "playing" with his wife. "Abimelech, king of the Philistines, looking out through a window, saw Isaac playing with Rebecca, his wife."

Now "Isaac" according to the allegorical interpretation of the Alexandrian commentators means "laughter" (cf. Gen. 21. 6) while "Rebecca" means "perseverance" (γέλως and ὑπομονή). Perseverance and laughter play with one another and it is thus that King Abimelech recognizes that they are indeed a wedded pair. We may think this a very far-fetched sort of allegory, yet it was the starting-point of a whole fascinating complex of ideas concerning the heavenly child's play of man, who can only be a true *Homo ludens* if he can unite gaiety with patience. Philo of Alexandria was the first to use this allegory as a vehicle for conveying his thoughts about life as a game: "True wisdom is never scowling or severe," he says, "nor is it full of worry and misgivings. On the contrary, it is gay and friendly, full of heartsease and joy. These qualities have moved many a man to witty jest, yet behind such jesting countertones of gravity and dignity must be audible, blending into a single harmonious whole, like the music of a well-tuned lyre." This, first and foremost, is a re-formulation of the Greek ideal of the "grave-merry" man, an ideal opposed to the early Stoic rigour that denied to the wise man any right whatsoever to gaiety or gladness of any kind. True wisdom smiles—precisely because it is serious. But now there comes into the Jewish sage's mind that biblical scene of the play between laughter and perseverance, with a king looking on. "According to Moses the end of wisdom is sport and laughter, not after the manner of the childish and unthinking, but after that of those who have grown grey, if not in years, at least in the good disposition of their souls. . . . Here we have Isaac whose name means 'laughter' for whom it is only right and proper to play with 'perseverance', as the Hebrews call 'Rebecca'. Yet such divine jesting of the soul must not be witnessed by any ordinary man but only by a king, . . . Abimelech. The latter looked through the window, by which is meant the soul's eye which sees into the open light beyond, and beheld Isaac playing with Rebecca his wife. For what could be more fitting for a wise man than to play, to be merry and glad of heart when perseverance in the good was at his side?"[1]

Somewhat more than a hundred years after this had been written, Clement of Alexandria worked these same ideas into the edifice of the new faith. The king watching the playing between laughter and perseverance became

[1] Philo, *De Plantatione*, 167–70 (Cohn–Wendland, II, pp. 167–8).

the Logos, Eternal Wisdom, laughter's wedded helpmate became perseverance in Christ, and in the playing
man he saw the man newly reborn of God. The Platonic
expression about the παιδιά of life is also consecrated and
hallowed and the whole passage from Genesis turned
into a mystery, the mystery of the playing child of God.
" 'Isaac' ", writes Clement, "should be translated
'laughter'. His playing with his wife Rebecca is witnessed
by the inquisitive king. His name was Abimelech, and
I cannot doubt that he stands for that sovereign Wisdom
which perceives the real inwardness of the mystery of
such play (τῆς παιδιᾶς τὸ μυστήριον). 'Rebecca' should
be translated as 'perseverance'." Whereupon Clement
breaks into a hymn in what is really a sacral metre:

> ὢ τῆς φρονίμου παιδιᾶς,
> γέλως δὶ ὑπομονῆς βοηθούμενος
> καὶ ἔφορος ὁ βασιλεύς.
> ἀγαλλιᾶται τὸ πνεῦμα
> τῶν ἐν Χριστῷ παιδίων
> ἐν ὑπομονῇ πολιτευομένων
> καὶ αὕτη ἡ θεία παιδιά.[1]

(Oh, the wisdom of this playing!
Perseverance the ally of laughter—
and all witnessed by the king!
Joyful is the spirit of those
who are children in Christ
and order their lives with patient perseverance.
This indeed is the playing of the children of God!)

The spirit of this Christian Greek who has just laid
down the wisdom of Hellas at the feet of his teacher,
Christ, turns back for a moment to that dim, far-off

[1] Clement Al., *Paedagogus*, I, 5, 21, 3-4 (*GCS* I, pp. 102-3).

pagan intuition of a God that played, and of which I too have had cause to speak in this book. Then his eyes gaze into the future and he sees how man, having once more become a child in God and played to the end with laughter and perseverance the game of his earthly life, joins his playing to that of Divine Wisdom at the celestial feast. "It is", he says, "such playing as this that Heraclitus attributes to his Zeus; and what more fitting for the wise and perfect man than to play and rejoice in the patient perseverance of good men and the administration of all good things, joining together and making merry in a common feast to God?"[1]

[1] Ibid., I, 5, 22, 1 (p. 103, ll. 6–9).

III

The Playing of the Church

I HAVE spoken of the playing of God and of the playing of man. Now we can go forward along an unexpected path leading right into the innermost dark heart of Christian revelation; for the God of Creation, whose work we were permitted to call a game, because it was both full of meaning and yet bound by no dictate of necessity, this same God of Creation has devoted himself—nay, has delivered himself—to his human creatures in a manner that surpasses in its nature any mere work of creating. He did this in becoming man and in all that great work of unconstrained and overflowing love which is linked with his incarnation and for which in its different aspects we have coined such words as grace, the Church and the beatific vision.

This tremendous outpouring, a happening in which the human mingles with the divine, has been called by me a game—and in this I have followed some of the most illustrious of Christian mystics—because there is, as I have said, nothing here of compulsion or calculation. This outpouring is a gift from God, which man, his creature, though a creature touched by grace, has no claim to receive, and the immensity of which is wholly beyond his capacity to measure; it is a gift proceeding in all its abundance from God's unique genius for love. And to this giving of himself by God man, as a child of God, can—and does—respond with a love that is equally uncalculating and free. Indeed, there is an even better

46

reason for calling this a game than for applying that term to the creation, for in this game of grace Christ has actually become the playmate of man, and when it is over, when the end has come of everything—faith, hope, law and sacrament—then there begins the divine children's game of the everlasting vision of God, the συμπανηγυρίζειν τῷ θεῷ, as Clement called it, the great panegyric in honour of God in which we all join together, the great festival of heaven.

Let us now seek to salvage some of those treasures so sadly neglected by our modern theologians with all their professorial earnestness. Let us do this with circumspection but with all the ardour and joy of one who is indeed diving for pearls.

First a point of semantics. The new relationship into which the Triune God entered with man when the Word was made flesh is the essence and sum of all mysteries. It is something so utterly beyond all philosophy that— as we have already seen—we can only speak of it in the dialectical terms of a negative, apophatic theology. Maximus the Confessor expounds this truth in his great dissertation on the playing of the Logos. When God himself breaks into our apparently closed order of play, something occurs that it is completely beyond the power of any human words to express. Then, we can only be like Paul and speak of the weakness and foolishness of God, or like the great doctor Gregory Nazianzen when he speaks of God's playing, knowing full well that such terms no more describe the full reality than if we were to speak of God's wisdom, power or earnestness. And this causes Maximus to say: "This children's game of which Gregory speaks is the incarnation, which so completely overrides (ὑπερουσίως) all the natural limits of

47

the natural order that, foreseeing it, the prophet David could say: 'In the greatness of thy strength shall thy enemies lie to thee' (Ps. 65. 3)."[1] This means that before the power of this mystery all attempts at positive and explicit description must prove completely futile and so we are driven to make use, as it were, of "lies", of words and images which by their very absurdity seem more apt to express the unfathomable riches of Divine Wisdom. This is precisely what we are doing when we refer to the order of grace that began with the incarnation as a children's game.

What I have principally to consider here, however, is the playing of the Church, and here once more we return to the symbolism woven round the theme of Isaac and Rebecca. The union of the Logos with our human nature in the womb of a virgin is a mystery of wedlock. The mothering womb is also the bridal chamber in which Christ is wedded to our human nature as a whole. The works of Augustine are full of this conception[2]—and Augustine is but one among many. Christ is the husband, our human nature is the wife, and there begins between them the wonderful love-play in which the wife is formed, cherished and redeemed so as to make of her the true bride whose name is *Ecclesia sancta*. This is the basic idea behind all theological symbolism, and in the light of it we can follow Clement of Alexandria as he carries this allegory of Isaac and Rebecca a stage further and extends the concept of *Homo ludens* beyond its personal application to the individual Christian until it reaches the theology of the playing of the Church.

[1] Maximus, *Ambigua*, 262a (*PG* 91, 1409CD).
[2] Augustine, *Confessiones*, IV, 12 (*CSEL* 33, p. 79, ll. 7–9); *Enarrationes in Psalmos*, 18, 6 (*PL* 36, 161). [Engl. tr. in *ACW*, 29.]

This Ecclesia is the true Eve, the helpmate of Adam. She is Rebecca (whose name means perseverance) and it is when the Logos who is Isaac (that is, laughter) is united with her that the game of redemption begins. "Again, it is possible", Clement continues in the same piece of exegesis, "to give a different interpretation to those indications which the Divine Wisdom has vouchsafed us in this story (Gen. 26. 8) and to show our understanding of its meaning by rejoicing and laughing over our salvation, just as Isaac did. But Isaac laughed because he had been delivered from death, playing and rejoicing with his bride, his helpmate in our salvation, who is, that is to say, the Church. But to her there is given an everlasting name, for she is called 'perseverance'. And this, because she alone, unceasingly rejoicing, will remain for ever, or because she is built up out of the perseverance of the faithful, that is of us, the members of Christ. The witness of those who have persevered to the end and the grateful joy the Church has in them—these things are the mystical children's game (μυστικὴ παιδιά)."[1]

Inspired by the same text, Augustine also deeply pondered this matter of the playing of the Church. He has set down his thoughts as follows: "The great patriarch [Isaac] played with his wedded wife, and it was made apparent by this that the two were united in wedlock. We must surely discern here a reference to the mystery by which Christ is united to his Church. How then should we interpret this matter? Truly no man will get at the truth of it unless he carefully reflects on the meaning of the allegory which centres on this scriptural figure. Whoever does this will find that the true Isaac for a time concealed his majesty—in which, being of the divine

[1] Clement Al., *Paedagogus*, I, 5, 22, 1 (*GCS* I, p. 103, ll. 9–17).

49

nature, he was the equal of the Father—under the disguise of a servant; for only thus could our human weakness accept him, and it was his will to use this means to adapt himself to his spouse. This being so, is it strange—nay, is it not most marvellously appropriate for the pre-figuring of what was to come—that Isaac, this prophet of God, should have begun to play voluptuously so that his wife's love for him might thus be roused? After all, it was in order to dwell among us that the Word of God took on man's flesh."[1]

There is yet another text in the Old Testament which moved the Fathers to speak of the playing of the Church. In Zechariah 8. 5 we have a vision of the peace of the coming Messianic age and are told: "The streets of the city shall be full of boys and girls playing in the streets thereof." This peace, the peace of men who have been redeemed and become as children, has already begun within the Church, the true *Civitas Dei*. So Cyril of Alexandria interprets the text as follows: "Boys who have not yet attained man's estate, little girls—this means the multitude of those who are as little children (νηπιωτάτη ηληθύς), those who have only just received the faith. It is they who, with their spiritual leaping and dancing, make so beautiful this really holy city which is the Church. And to these we may surely apply the saying: 'Come, let us rejoice before God who is our salvation'."[2] The faith and joy in redemption that come to the baptized Christian, to him who has for ever become a child born of God, are, in fact, a real children's play and the Church is graced by the measures of a dance whose rhythm is set by the Holy Spirit.

[1] Augustine, *Contra Faustum Manichaeum*, XXII, 46 (*CSEL* 25, pp. pp. 638–9).

[2] Cyril Al., *Commentarius in Zachariam*, 40 (*PG* 72, 113B).

Jerome gives a similar meaning to the prophetic text: "May the streets of the city be full of boys and girls playing. This can only be when a city enjoys profound peace and security, for then even the young folk freely follow the motions of their hearts and join in the gladness of the State with dance and play. Now all this may be applied to the Church of whom it is written: 'Glorious things are said of thee, O city of God' (Ps. 86. 3). . . . For in her the joy of the spirit finds expression in bodily gesture and her children shall say with David as they dance the solemn step (*tripudiante saltatu*): 'I will dance and play before the face of the Lord' (II Kings [Sam.] 6. 22 [LXX])."[1]

This conception of the "playing Church" signifying the body of all those who have found gladness in Christ, has about it the quality of true poetry and is at the same time full of deep theological meaning. It was to be revived once more by a mind with a rare feeling for this kind of imagery. The author of the exquisite little verse that follows is Notker, the stammering monk of St Gall, who composed it for the solemnities of Easter, the Church's feast of spring:

> *Ecce sub vite*
> *amoena, Christe,*
> *ludet in pace*
> *omnis Ecclesia.*[2]
> (Lo, under the gentle
> vine, O Christ,
> the whole Church
> plays in peace.)

[1] Jerome, *Commentarii in Zachariam*, II, 8 (*PL* 25, 1465B f.).
[2] *Analecta Hymnica*, 53, p. 96, Leipzig, 1911.—Cf. Hugo Rahner, *Mater Ecclesia*, pp. 69 and 142, Einsiedeln, 1944.

But this mystical theology of the Church at play can be given still greater meaning and depth if we bring an idea to bear on it that arises from the very fact of God's having become man. It is an idea already implicit in Jerome's words which I have just quoted and which I should like to set as a motto at the head of this chapter. "In the Church the joy of the spirit finds expression in bodily gesture." Now, whatever view you may take of the Catholic Church and its claims, it is one of the fundamental facts of our spiritual and cultural history that this Church, which bases her whole thinking on her faith that God put on human flesh and appeared amongst us, has maintained intact the unity between mind and body, between idea and symbol, between the unseen and the seen. All earthly things have for her retained the quality of mystery. She uses visible things such as the sun, the moon, water, wine and oil, but teaches our spiritual eye to see beyond their outward form, beyond the mere foreground of history, and penetrate to the purposes of God, to the truths that endure for ever. She is one coherent sacrament.

The incursion of divine life into the world, first in the spoken word of Holy Writ, and then, at the end of time, in the Logos himself, is an event ever new. It is a happening she can always grasp afresh, a parable told by God himself. Audible and tangible in the immediate, pregnant further with mysteries no man can utter. That is precisely the reason why she can look upon the whole visible creation as an unceasing game played by God, as a "bodily gesture" expressing at every moment the joy of the Holy Ghost.

Philo had perceived this when he wrote, speaking of the marvels worked by God in the course of Israel's

history: "Anyone who does not believe this, obviously
knows nothing of God and has not yet sought after him.
Had he done so, he would have known and understood
that all these extraordinary (παράδοξα) and unreasonable
things (παράλογα) are merely God's playthings (θεοῦ
παίγνια). To convince himself of this it would be enough
to contemplate the great and really serious works of
God—the heavens, the stars and the earth."[1] God makes
himself known as a revealing God in the works, both
equally unreasonable, of miracle and foolishness, and
that is how he plays. Everything that meets our gaze is
a parable veiling and unveiling its higher meaning, a
truth to which we see that Eusebius is alive when he says
of the great catch of fish: "This is all no more than a
children's game and a figure for what is to come."[2]

Now all this applies to the earthly forms of the Church
herself, to the sacraments as visible signs of invisible
grace, and to the playing which is her liturgy. What
occurs in baptism, says Bede, in the mysterious birth
from water and the Spirit, is a mystery of which our
knowledge is only by faith; seen from the outside it is
no more than mere colourful play-acting. "*Sola haec
Ecclesia Mater, quae generat, novit. Ceterum oculis inspicientium
videtur talis exire de fonte qualis intravit, totumque ludus esse
videtur quod agitur* – Only Mother Church who has given
birth to this thing, knows what is taking place. Apart
from that, to the eyes of the beholder the person appears
to come out of the baptismal font the same as he went in,
and all that is done seems no more than a piece of play."[3]
Here are the theological grounds for what Guardini has

---

[1] Philo, *Vita Moysis*, I, 212 (Cohn–Wendland, IV, p. 171, ll. 6–10).
[2] Eusebius, *Syrian Theophany*, IV, 6 (*GCS* III, 2, p. 172, ll. 31–2).
[3] Bede, *Homiliae*, II, 12 (*PL* 94, 198D).

to say about the liturgy as a divine game.[1] Indeed this Church, the Church of the Logos made man, will always clothe her deepest mystery in a visible cloak of beautiful gesture, of measured steps and noble raiment. Everlastingly she will be the Church that plays, for she takes the physical, the flesh, man in fact, with a divine seriousness.

With this as our starting-point, we can gain some understanding of a doctrine which, though something of a stranger in the teaching of the schools, was all the more zealously cultivated in the secret cells of the mystics. It is the teaching that God's election by grace is a game.

The Christian mystic—and it is of the Christian mystic alone that I am speaking—is one who sees through visible things and perceives the inexpressible that lies beyond. When he looks upon the cross of his Lord, then, behind the tortured foolishness of what he beholds, there opens to him the wide and shining vista of security in God's grace and redemption; there begins between the depths of his soul and the great heart of God that *commercium admirabile* which he feels and experiences as "the playing of grace". Bede expressed this feeling in a poem on the holy cross:

> *En ludus est credentium*
> *tuis frui complexibus*
> *quae tanta gignis gaudia*
> *pandis polique ianuas.*[2]
> (It is as play for the faithful
> to enjoy thy embraces
> for thou begettest such great joys
> and openest the gates of heaven.)

[1] Romano Guardini, *The Spirit of the Liturgy* (tr. Ada Lane), pp. 85–106: "The Playfulness of the Liturgy", London, 1937.

[2] *Analecta Hymnica*, 50, p. 112, Leipzig, 1907.—Bede, *Hymni*, 13 (*PL* 94, 633c).

54

This favour of God's grace is felt by the mystic to be a divine game, for it is as if all doors were suddenly thrown open, as though in a wholly unmerited fashion he were snatched up into a lover's embrace. In it is repeated in the core of the soul what once took place in the depths of the Triune God when, as an act of gratuitous love, the resolve was made that man should be redeemed, and the game of the incarnation was begun. Mechtild of Magdeburg very boldly describes the making of this loving resolve: "Then the Holy Ghost made play for the Father with great gentleness . . . and said: 'Lord, dear Father, we would no longer be unfruitful.' "[1] And this loving resolve is still active. That is why the mystic experiences his surrender to grace as though it were an immersion in the flood of an entirely new freedom, as a handing over of himself to a love that knows no bounds, as a kind of release from all constraint such as we can only imagine in the heart of a child. And so quite naturally we return to the idea of play. Mechtild begs our Lord's humanity to "open to her that swirling flood that plays within the Trinity by which alone the soul can live".[2] And God says to her: "The soul shall experience my blessedness . . . if it will lay itself trustfully in my divine arms, so that I must play with it."[3]

To the nun Altheit of Trochau Christ says: "I will to make thee a very great figure and thou wouldst be the most mighty of prioresses that ever was in this

[1] *The Revelations of Mechtild of Magdeburg* (1210–1297) *or the Flowing Light of the Godhead* (tr. Lucy Menzies), III, 9, pp. 74–5, London, 1953. [In this and the following extracts, the text as given here is not always taken from the English work referred to. We have followed Fr Rahner's version which he describes as "quoted according to the text in Gall Morel, *Die Offenbarungen der Mechtild von Magdeburg*, p. 111, Rogensburg, 1869".—*Translator.*]

[2] Ibid., IV, 12 (Morel, p. 175; Menzies, p. 105).

[3] Ibid., V, 25 (Morel, p. 278; Menzies, p. 152).

convent and also the most blessed, but then I could no longer play my play of grace with thee as I used to do. Now choose as thou wilt." And Altheit said: "My Lord, thy grace I can never forgo."[1]

How comes it that the mystic can thus speak of the playing of grace? It is because in doing so he touches the deepest of theological mysteries, that of God's election by grace. He knows from experience that God grants his love with sovereign freedom, from time everlasting predetermining the nature of this gift without in any way impairing the creature's spiritual freedom; that in all this he is incalculable and unpredictable and yet infinitely purposeful. Because of this knowledge, the mystic knows that he has but to plunge into this abyss and that in doing so he will never lose himself; he knows that he may be childlike and even foolish. For the fundamental rule of this divine game is: "He who loses, wins"; and so it was set down by the Spanish mystic and Jesuit lay-brother, Alphonsus Rodriguez, in the treatise, both childlike and profound, on "God's play with the soul".[2] What outwardly appears as fate, suffering or, spoken in Christian terms, as a participation in the seemingly senseless annihilation upon the cross, is, for the mystic who sees through all the outer coverings of things, the wonderfully calculated playing of an everlasting love, thought out and elaborated with a care for detail of which love alone is capable. "The playing of God is different in different people," says the mystic Venturino da Bergamo.[3]

---

[1] Die Nonne von Engeltal, *Büchlein von der Gnaden Überlast* (ed. M. Weinhandl), pp. 278–9, Munich, 1921.

[2] A. Rodriguez, *Die Vereinigung der Seele mit Jesus Christus*. Geistliche Abhandlungen (ed. Prinz Max, Herzog zu Sachsen), pp. 234–53: "Gottes Spiele mit der Seele – God's Games with the Soul", Freiburg, 1907.

[3] W. Oehl, *Deutsche Mystikerbriefe des Mittelalters*, p. 293, Munich, 1931.

From all that has been said of the mystic's utter surrender, it surely is clear that we are dealing with something much greater than the pretty conceit of a little nun when Teresa of Lisieux expresses her desire to be nothing more than a toy, a little ball for the child Jesus, "a toy of no value—a ball say—such as a child might throw on the ground or leave lying in a corner, or press to his heart if he feels that way about it".[1] These words are not to be taken lightly; they represent a fundamental and properly evangelical understanding of the nature of grace. Here on this highest human level, in the region of sanctity that is to say, we again encounter that unity between seriousness and play of which Plato had already been dimly aware, and we learn that it means to do all things and yet to account oneself as nothing, even as our Lord enjoined: "When you shall have done all these things that are commanded you, say: We are unprofitable servants" (Luke 17. 10).

This mysticism of the play of grace, as Teresa of Lisieux describes it, made a particularly profound impression on a Chinese Christian thinker who wrote the following words: "Like Shakespeare and Lao Tse, Teresa is so simple and yet so perceptive that she succeeds in finding her way back to naïveté, for she knows the value of folly."[2] And surely Walter Nigg was right when he says of this wish to be a plaything of God that it "betokens a music of the heart which only a saint can command".[3] The most serious part of the Christian ideal of

[1] Teresa of Lisieux, *Autobiography of a Saint* (tr. Ronald Knox), p. 171, London, 1958.—We find the same thought in a mystic of our own day: H. Braun, *Der namenlose Gott*, pp. 71–84, Munich, 1938.

[2] John Wu-Kien-Yong, *Die Wissenschaft der Liebe.* Das Glaubensbekenntnis eines östlichen Christen (ed. D. Thalhammer), p. 34, Freiburg i. Br., 1944.

[3] Walter Nigg, *Grosse Heilige*, pp. 402–3, Zurich, 1946.

57

man is to be found in the fact that he who has faith and
truly loves God is also the man who can truly play, for
only he who is secure in God can be truly light of heart.
I cull from the hidden treasures of this wonderful anthro-
pology of the playing of man some words of an Eastern
monk. I choose them because I know nothing that expresses
with greater beauty or with greater precision the innermost secret of the Christian σπουδγέλοιος: "To shorten
one's sleep at night, to exploit to the full every hour of
the day, to use oneself to the bone and then understand
that it is all a jest—that is to be serious indeed."[1]

I have still a word to add, for Church and grace are
but an earthly prelude to that final consummation which
is the eternal beginning—the blessed vision of God. They
are indeed a *"praeludium"*, for—let us say it again—all
earthly things are but a game, a children's game, however serious and decisive they may appear, compared
with that secure harmony of body and soul which we call
heaven.

Yet, as was pointed out earlier, this playing here on
earth, whether we conceive of it as an activity or a state
of mind, is but a feeble and tentative imitation of what is
in store for us, and the Christian has never ceased to use
the concept of play as a verbal figure that most aptly
describes, as far as he is able to conceive it, the state of
the blessed in the world to come. There is a saying of
Heraclitus that "before the divine, man is as a child,
even as a boy is before a man".[2] This utterance by that
obscure spirit from Ephesus prompted Eusebius to say
some deeply pondered things about the game eternity is,
a game for which we prepare ourselves here below, like

[1] Cf. J. Bernhart, *Der stumme Jubel*, p. 108, Graz–Vienna, 2nd edn. 1947.
[2] Fragment 79 (Diels, *Fragmente der Vorsokratiker*, I, p. 169).

an infant in its mother's womb—and indeed, like the latter, always with the possibility of a miscarriage. Like the latter, we are at one and the same time secure and imperilled. But let Eusebius speak for himself and let us note especially how he conceives of the nature of the life in store for us when we have left the womb and become spiritual adults in heaven: Our earthly life, he writes, is like that of an infant in its mother's womb as compared with that of a fully grown man; for in this world man, whatever his perfections, is like a child when compared with the adult angels. He who has a faulty posture while in this earthly womb and cannot be successfully born is one who will never "see the joyous faces of those angels or hear their laughter".[1] Our true playing and our true merriment will only begin when this world has been left behind.

That is something that was already dimly apprehended by pious men among the pagan Greeks. There is a Greek vase on which Eros is depicted merrily playing ball with a maiden. The superscription reads: "ἵησάν μοι τὰν σφαῖραν – The ball has been thrown to me." Surely Bachofen is right when he discerns a belief in a life of bliss in another world behind this pictorial symbolism: "Behind this cheerful game there is concealed the most exalted hope of the mystery."[2] Certainly the devotees of Adonis looked forward to light-hearted, everlasting games in the meadows of heaven. "*Laetus Adoneis lusibus insereris,*" runs a line of the epitaph of the young initiate, Marcus Lucceus, "Joyfully thou wilt enter into the games of Adonis"[3], while in the syncretistic painting in the

---

[1] Eusebius, *Syrian Theophany*, I, 72 (*GCS* III, 2, p. 73, ll. 25–6).
[2] J. J. Bachofen, *Urreligion und Symbole*, pp. 477–8.
[3] H. Hepding, *Attis, seine Mythen und sein Kult*, p. 92, Giessen, 1903.

59

catacombs, the Paradise of Vibia, the blessed play the game of knuckle-bones which they had so loved while on earth.[1]

All this may appear childish enough, yet how can a religious man express the nature of what he hopes for in the life to come save through the inadequate medium of visual images and words? He hopes for freedom, rest, release from all preoccupation of mind, for untroubled gladness of soul; he longs to be once more a child, a child in utter security, and, like a child, to play; he hopes, in a word, for that complete heartsease that will allow even his body, freed now from the burden of its earthly life, to move and sway to the measures of a heavenly dance.

The Christian of antiquity was no exception to all this. He too starts talking of playing and dancing when he seeks clumsily and inadequately to describe the bliss of heaven in terms of human speech, and on his sarcophagi are little cherubs playing with hoops.[2] The epitaph of Beratius Niketoras, a Christian of the early fourth century, portrays paradise in a kind of hymnal ecstasy: "I will sing praises to thee and dance with the choirs of saints."[3] And when the poet Prudentius sings of the innocent infants of Bethlehem and of their heavenly bliss, he is driven to express his thought in the charming little verse:

> *Aram ante ipsam simplices*
> *palma et coronis luditis.*[4]

[1] Cf. F. Cumont, *Die orientalischen Religionen im römischen Heidentum*, p. 60 and pl. I, 4. [Engl. tr.: *The Oriental Religions in Roman Paganism*. With an introductory essay by Grant Showerman.]—M. J. Rostovtzeff, *Mystic Italy*, p. 146, New York, 1927.

[2] Cf. *Dictionnaire d'Archéologie chrétienne et de Liturgie* (=*DACL*), VII, 2, s.v. "Jeux et jouets", fig. 6255, Paris, 1927.

[3] J. Quasten, *Die Grabinschrift des Beratius Niketoras* (Mitteilungen des deutschen Archäologischen Instituts, Römische Abteilung, 53), p. 61, Münster, 1938.—T. K. Kempf, *Christus der Hirt*, p. 195, Rome, 1942.

[4] Prudentius, *Cathemerinon*, XII, 131–2 (*CSEL* 61, p. 73).

(With palm branches and wreaths ye play,
ye innocent creatures, before the very altar of God.)

It is almost as if Prudentius, himself a Spaniard, were distraining in advance on the art of Murillo.

The most moving evidence, however, of this ancient Christian mysticism of play comes from the Acts of the two Carthaginian martyrs, Perpetua and Felicitas. The following words are those of the editor (who may well have been Tertullian) of the diary-like records of the martyr Saturus. The latter in a vision beholds the entry of the two women into paradise. They are carried by four angels to the throne of God, whom they see as a "man with snow-white hair and a youthful face" and who strokes their cheeks by way of divine greeting. Beside the throne stand four elders who say to the newcomers: "*Ite et ludite* – go and play!" Then Saturus says to Perpetua: "Now thou hast what thou didst desire", and Perpetua concludes this heavenly colloquy by saying: "*Deo gratias, ut quomodo in carne hilaris fui, hilarior sum et hic modo* – Thanks be to God! As I was merry in the flesh, now here I am merrier still."[1] This vision of an African Christian of the early third century exactly expresses what straightforward religious men of all ages have felt and hoped for whenever they have thought about the life to come. The faith of the Christian gives him the certainty that all this will one day be his, for he knows that it is assured through the God who became man and is carrying on his game of grace.

---

[1] "Passio SS. Felicitatis et Perpetuae", 12, in Rudolf Knopf and Gustav Krüger, *Ausgewählte Märtyrerakten* (Sammlung ausgewählter kirchen- und dogmengeschichtlicher Quellenschriften, N. F., 3), pp. 40–1, Tübingen, Mohr, 1929. [Engl. tr. in, e.g.: *Faithful Witnesses: Records of Early Christian Martyrs* (ed. E. R. Hardy) (World Christian Books, 31), London, 1960.]

Heaven will be a game, because it will then be permitted to man to attain a condition which the mystic Mechtild of Magdeburg has described with all the pregnancy of true poetic and religious genius: "There we shall be glad and free, lively, strong and clear, and as far as may be, like unto God."[1] This playing in heaven will be the Holy Ghost's game, an everlasting movement in rhythm with the Spirit which "bloweth where it listeth". Here are some lines (which are quoted in modern German) in which the great mistress of words from Magdeburg sings the delights of this heavenly play:

> *Der Heilige Geist giesst auch*
> *in Fülle aus seiner Minne Fluss,*
> *womit er Gnade den Seligen schenkt*
> *und sie mit solcher Fülle tränkt,*
> *dass sie mit Freuden singen,*
> *lieblich lachen und springen,*
> *in sanfter Weise fliessen und schwimmen*
> *und fliegen und klimmen*
> *von Chor zu Chor*
> *bis zu des Reiches Höhen empor.*[2]

> (Here too the Spirit shafts
> Such heavenly floods of light
> On all the Blest that they,
> Filled and enchanted, sing
> For joy, and laugh and leap
> In ordered dance. They flow
> And swim and fly and climb
> From tierèd choir to choir
> Still upward through the heights.)

[1] Mechtild of Magdeburg, VII, 1 (Morel, p. 391; Menzies, p. 208?).
[2] Ibid. (Menzies, p. 209, cited verbatim).

This is really the end of my essay on the theology of heavenly play. Man redeemed has once more become a child, even as he was at the time of his earthly birth and of his begetting out of the Church's primal sacrament. A child once more, he plays. He is taken up into the "choir of blessed boys", even as Goethe, at the end of his *Faust*, had reverently conceived that it would be. Transformed and released from the limitations of his previous chrysalis-like existence he enters into eternal youth:

> *Sieh, wie er jedem Erdenbande*
> *der alten Hülle sich entrafft,*
> *und aus ätherischem Gewande*
> *hervortritt erste Jugendkraft.*[1]
> (Behold, how he each band hath cloven,
> The earthly life hath round him thrown,
> And through his garb, of ether woven,
> The early force of youth is shown!)

The end will be even as the beginning—an eternal childhood. For the child at play is always an irreducible duality of weakness and strength, of earnest and jest. "The 'child' ", says Jung, "is all that is abandoned and exposed and at the same time divinely powerful; the insignificant, dubious beginning, and the triumphal end. The 'eternal child' in man is an indescribable experience, an incongruity, a disadvantage, and a divine prerogative; an imponderable that determines the ultimate worth or worthlessness of a personality."[2]

The child in man desires to play—and the final answer to that longing, the answer of truth to all our searchings,

---

[1] Goethe, *Faust*, Part II, Act V, Scene vii, ll. 245–8. [Engl. tr. by Bayard Taylor in The World's Classics, 380, p. 389, London, n.d.]
[2] Jung–Kerényi, *Essays on a Science of Mythology*, p. 135 (by Jung).

is the word of him who being himself the Word, became a little child: "Unless you become as little children, you shall not enter into the kingdom of heaven" (Matt. 18. 3). That is why the streets of the heavenly city will be full of playing children and the Ancient of Days, whose face is for ever young, will never cease to say to men: "*Ite et ludite*."

IV

The Heavenly Dance

ALL that I have really attempted so far has been to set
before you a study of the significance of play written
from the point of view of an historian of religion. I think
I have made at least one thing clear. It is that in the last
analysis there is a secret, a mystery, at the heart of every
form of play, and that in it all, from the playing of
children to the playing in heaven, there is one intent—
the blessed seriousness of which, as Plato saw long ago,
God alone is worthy. All play, wrote Plotinus, is secretly
directed towards θεωρία; it arises from the longing for the
vision of the divine; for in play all that is gay, lovely and
soaring in the human spirit strives to find the expression
which a man of the spirit and of enthusiasm is ever
seeking to attain. There is a sacral secret at the root and
in the flowering of all play: it is man's hope for another
life taking visible form in gesture.

To play is to yield oneself to a kind of magic, to enact
to oneself the absolutely other, to pre-empt the future,
to give the lie to the inconvenient world of fact. In play
earthly realities become, of a sudden, things of the transient
moment, presently left behind, then disposed of and
buried in the past; the mind is prepared to accept the
unimagined and incredible, to enter a world where
different laws apply, to be relieved of all the weights
that bear it down, to be free, kingly, unfettered and divine.
Man at play is reaching out—as has already been said—
for that superlative ease, in which even the body, freed

from its earthly burden, moves to the effortless measures
of a heavenly dance.

With this thought we enter a world of ideas, the
discussion of which will form a kind of epilogue to what
I have been saying on the subject of *Theologia ludens*.
All play has somewhere deep within it an element of the
dance; it is a kind of dance round the truth. Sacral play
has always taken the form of a dance; for in the rhythm
of body and music are conjoined all the possibilities of
embodying and expressing in visible form the strivings
and aspirations of the mind—and also, of chastely veiling
and protecting them. The Greeks used the dance to give
just such concealed and cryptic expression to the ἄρρητά,
the unspeakable things of the mysteries; for they knew
that there are certain insights and intimations which go
beyond the powers of speech and may only be expressed
in some kind of comely action. Indeed so intimately
linked was the dance with the mysteries that any offence
against the mysteries tended to be described in terms of
the dance. Thus anyone who spoke of the mysteries in a
frivolous manner or on an unsuitable occasion was said
to ἐξορχεῖσθαι the mysteries, to be "dancing them away"
or "dancing the mystery out of them", and this word still
meant just as much to such men as Clement and Dionysius; as well it might, for there were Christian mysteries
as well as pagan ones and only a soul inspired could even
begin to grasp their meaning. On such things reverent
silence must be observed. "It is indeed perilous", so it is
written in the *Stromata*, "to 'dance away' (i.e. to babble
out) the truly inexpressible teaching of the only real
'philosophy'."[1] It is only in the ultimate vision of God,

[1] Clement Al., *Stromata*, I, 2, 21, 2 (*GCS* II, p. 14, ll. 13–15).—Cf. H.
Koch, *Pseudo-Dionysius Areopagita in seinen Beziehungen zum Neuplatonismus
und Mysterienwesen, pp.* 116ff., Mainz, 1900.

when, according to Hippolytus, the Logos is "the holy leader of the dance", that man redeemed will join in the easy rhythms of truth and that, as we are told in the epitaph of Niketoras, we shall "dance with the choirs of the saints".

Let us then seek to catch a few of the words of wisdom uttered by both Greeks and Christians concerning this theology of the dance.

The dance is a sacral form of play because it is, first and foremost, an attempt to imitate in the form of gesture and rhythm something of that free-soaring motion which God as creative principle has imparted to the cosmos. Plotinus says somewhere that the pattern of the world is "the truest work of poetry, which men with poetic gifts partially recreate in poetry of their own. It is the soul that speaks the lines, and the lines to be spoken are given it by the supreme ποιητής", a word with the double significance of poet and maker. The more the human mind penetrates into the secrets of the universe, either by intuitive feeling or by clear understanding, the better fitted a man becomes for moving in time with the divine, "for the true activity of life is that of the artist, such as the dancer in motion who is indeed the image and symbol thereof".[1]

Plotinus is led by these reflections to develop the conception of his great "world theatre". The proceeding of the cosmos from out the "one" of the divine, and its adornment, are a drama, a contrapuntal reconciliation of opposites: it is a battle of elements, a "planned re-

---

[1] Plotinus, *Enneads*, III, 2, 16 (ed. Harder, V, p. 45).—On the dance in Greek religion and the mysteries, cf. K. Latte, *De Saltationibus Graecorum Capita Quinque* (Religionsgeschichtliche Versuche und Vorarbeiten, 13, 3), Giessen, 1913; K. Prümm, *Religionsgeschichtliches Handbuch für den Raum der altchristlichen Umwelt*, pp. 487–8, Freiburg, 1943.

lationship of notes". Man who, while here below feels hemmed in by this veritable *concertatio*, must strain every sense to catch the rhythm of the whole.

Philo too, though he strikes a more Stoic note and is certainly influenced by Plato's conceit, uses the image of the marionettes, the θαύμαρα, and also talks of the "dance" of life. He who thus dances in this mortal life must use his senses to discover "who it is that, invisibly and while himself remaining invisible, imparts motion to this wonderful puppet-show by pulling the strings (νευροσπαστῶν ἀόρατος ἀοράτως)".[1] Through the world of the senses man who is part of this cosmic eurythmic gains the knowledge that he is actually dancing in step with the world when he has brought his body into time with his soul, or—to put the matter differently—when the soul can make the body so subservient to it that word, gesture and tone of voice become a true expression of the spirit.

Lucian of Samosata has left us a little book on the dance that should certainly not be taken more seriously than was intended by the fashionable *littérateur* who was its author. Yet with its jesting it mingles real depth of thought. Under the cloak of pure fun and with the lightest of touches, its author says many things that are both serious and profoundly true. It is in fact a kind of Mozartian *opéra bouffe* in classical costume.

The dance, declares Lucian, is much more than a mere pleasure. Rather is it a form of activity that is of great profit to the soul, for it "brings the souls of men into the right rhythm and shows forth in visible fashion what the inner beauty of the soul has in common with the outer beauty of the body, because it makes manifest the point

---

[1] Philo, *De Fuga et Inventione*, 45 and 46 (Cohn–Wendland, III, pp. 119–20).

where the two flow into one another".[1] And so, he argues
later on, a man can only dance correctly and with beauty
if he knows human nature and so is truly wise. The
dancer must have that quality which Thucydides praised
in Pericles: "γνῶναί τε τὰ δέοντα καὶ ἑρμηνεῦσαι αὐτά –
to know that which rightly should be and interpret it".
He, therefore, speaks of the dance as the art of incarnating
the spiritual and making visible the invisible. Finally he
defines the art of dance in terms of three concepts:

ἐπιστήμη μιμητικὴ καὶ δεικτική,
τῶν ἐννοηθέντων ἐξαγορευτική,
τῶν ἀφανῶν σαφηνιστική.[2]

It is an

imitative and demonstrative technique,
proclaiming what is in the mind,
and making manifest what is unseen.

Lesbonax of Mytilene, therefore, according to Lucian,
had said a profoundly true thing when he called the
dancer χειρόσοφος – wise with his hands.[3]

In his definitions, of course, Lucian touches the innermost secret of every art, for every art strives, through
endless failures, to give to the unseen that visible form
that is somehow "just right". All artists are in perpetual
pursuit of this secret: these men possessed by the spirit,
who, in sound, in colour or by gesture, venture the
attempt of uttering the unutterable, and who, in that
rare moment, seem suddenly, though but for an instant,
to have attained their desire, feel playing around them
the smile of divinity, the smile that is a reflection of the

[1] Lucian, *De Saltatione*, 6 (Jacobitz [Bibliotheca Teubneriana], II,
p. 146).
[2] Ibid., 36 (p. 156).
[3] Ibid., 69 (p. 164).

Divine Wisdom playing upon the earth. "For any classical gesture in which a culture finds expression," says the *ludimagister* of the *Glasperlenspiel*, "has in its ultimate analysis a moral connotation, it is an exemplary model for human conduct concentrated into gesture form."[1] And like music the dance expresses knowledge "of the tragedy of human destiny; . . . it affirms acceptance of human destiny and courage in face of it; . . . it carries with it a sound of that superhuman laughter in which there is everlasting mirth".[2] Who can help thinking of the charm of Mozart's music that seems to rise out of his tears? And who can help calling to mind Rilke's fifth *Duino Elegy* which under the figure of the street acrobats of a Paris suburb makes plain the contrast between the pitiful virtuosity that has been painfully acquired and the divine moment in which for once the artist's intention assumes a perfect bodily form. There it is—the same immortal saying about laughter and the dance, and in it the angel is adjured to preserve this creation of a single moment as in an urn full of precious healing herbs:

> *Und dennoch blindlings,*
> *das Lächeln . . .*
> *Engel! o nimms, pflücks, das kleinblütige Heilkraut.*
> *Schaff eine Vase, verwahrs! Stells unter jene uns noch nicht*
> *offenen Freuden; in lieblicher Urne*
> *rühms mit blumiger, schwungiger Aufschrift:*
> *"Subrisio saltat".*[3]

(And still, all instinctive,
that smile . . . .

---

[1] "*Den eine Moral letzten Endes bedeutet jede klassische Kulturgebärde, ein zur Gebärde zusammengezogenes Vorbild des menschlichen Verhaltens.*"

[2] Hermann Hesse, *Das Glasperlenspiel*, I, p. 65.

[3] Leipzig, 1931, p. 25. [Engl. tr.: Rainer Maria Rilke, *Selected Works*, vol. II, *Poetry* (tr. J. B. Leishman), p. 235, London, 1960.]

Angel! oh, take it, pluck it, that small-flowered herb
of healing!
Get a vase to preserve it. Set it among those joys
not yet open to us: in a graceful urn
praise it, with florally soaring inscription:
"Subrisio saltat".)

The poor "artiste" represents the artist and the healing
herb is that perfection of his art which for the present is
unattainable, but of which for a moment he catches a
distant glimpse—the creation of that inimitable thing
that is wholly beyond mere technique, the thing that
soars aloft from the earth or, to quote the words at the
end of the elegy, the "daring lofty figures of heart-
flight, their towers of pleasure – *die kühnen hohen Figuren
des Herzschwungs, ihre Türme aus Lust*". But the moment
this technique really for an instant—and only for a single
instant—"brings it off", the divine sun breaks through
the darkness and then we may indeed say: "*Subrisio
saltatoris* – the dancer's smile*".
The harmony between the artist's body and soul
which is the ultimate mystery of the dance is, however,
but part of a larger whole, for in the dance there is also
a cosmic mystery. It is an attempt to move in time with
that creative love that "made the sun and the other
stars". It is once again Lucian, that "serious-merry" man,
who writes: "Those who most accurately describe the
genealogy of the dancer's art, declare that its origin is
the same as that of the world itself, and that it appeared
together with that primal eros that is the beginning of all
things; for what is that dance of the stars, what is that
regular intertwining of the planets with the fixed stars,
what are the common measure and sweet harmonies of

their movements—what are all these things but repetitions of that great dance that was in the beginning (πρωτόγονος ὄρχησις)?"

It is this cosmic dance that the mysteries seek to imitate, and that, it was alleged, is why, when people wish to say that someone has "babbled out" the mysteries, they often use a word meaning that he had "danced them out of time or improperly".[1]

The people of antiquity were quite familiar with the idea of the dance of the stars and used this expression to convey their sense of the loveliness of the sparkling firmament. "The fixed stars", says Philo, "dance a truly divine dance because they never depart from the order which the all-begetting Father has directed them to observe in the cosmos."[2] The name "The Dancers" was actually applied to one particular constellation which the Romans knew as "The Players".[3] Chalcidius tells us that "the planets are carried by a balanced and wonderfully harmonious motion and this is why Plato calls it a dance",[4] and Claudius Claudianus in an epithalamium in which he conjures up something very like the atmosphere of a fairy tale tells how on the bride's wedding day milk and wine came bubbling forth from the earth, and the chariot of Helios came to a standstill. Then we are told: "*tunc exultasse choreis astra ferunt* – then men say the stars rejoiced with dances."[5] Christian poets use much

---

[1] Lucian, *De Saltatione*, 7 (Jacobitz, II, p. 147), and 15 (p. 150).

[2] Philo, *De Cherubim*, 23 (Cohn–Wendland, I, p. 175, ll. 16–17).

[3] The stars of the Little Bear.—Cf. Hyginus, *Poetica Astronomica*, III, 1, and Germanicus, *Scholia Strozziana* (Breysig, p. 115).–See on this F. Boll, *Sphaera*, p. 259, Leipzig, 1903.

[4] Chalcidius, *Translatio Platonis Timaei* (Wrobel, p. 124).

[5] Claudius Claudianus, *Carmina*, XXI, 84–5 (Monumenta Germaniae Historica, Auctores Antiqui, X, p. 192).

the same language. "The stars", says Claudianus Mamertus, "make colourful (*pingunt*) the sky with well-numbered choruses of dancers and harmonious intervals."[1]

Now it is one of the fundamental ideas of the astral mysticism of late antiquity that the souls of men are formed out of the essence of this world of the stars.[2] It was thought that this belief embodied some of the ancient wisdom of Heraclitus, as we can see from Macrobius' commentary on the *Somnium Scipionis*.[3] Indeed Cicero himself maintains in this same *Somnium* that played so important a part in the Christian Middle Ages, that "man has received his spirit from that fiery realm that you call the stars, those bodies which follow their courses with such marvellous swiftness".[4] Thither the souls also return, and it is the stars, according to the teaching of the Pythagoreans, that are the home of the blessed. And so, the soul that even here below seeks to be united to the divine, must seek to join in the dance of the stars, so that even in this present life it may be what it was originally and what it will be again. "For God desires", says Philo, "that the soul of the wise should be a copy of the heavens. Nay, if I may express myself under the form of a paradox, it should be an οὐρανὸς ἐπίγειος – a heaven brought down to earth, so that it may have that within itself which is to be found in the ether, namely . . . ordered movement, well-measured dances (χορείας ἐμμελεῖς),

---

[1] Claudianus Mamertus, *De Statu Animae*, II, 12 (*CSEL*, 11, p. 149).

[2] Cf. F. Cumont, *Astrology and Religion among the Greeks and Romans*, New York, 1912; Idem, *Die orientalischen Religionen im römischen Heidentum*, pp. 126ff. [*The Oriental Religions in Roman Paganism*.]—E. Pfeiffer, *Studien zum antiken Sternglauben*, pp. 28ff.; 113-30, Leipzig, 1916.

[3] Macrobius, *In Somnium Scipionis*, I, 14, 19.—Cf. Diels, *Fragmente der Vorsokratiker*, 12, A 15.

[4] Cicero, *Somnium Scipionis*, 15 (=*De Republica*, VI, 15).

periodic cycles in divinely ordained rhythms, starlike rays of virtue that shine with brightest lustre."[1]

That men would tend to see in the dance a reflection of such "ordered movements", and that their intuitive feelings about it as a potentially religious vehicle would be strengthened by such ideas, is surely obvious enough. Certainly the people of antiquity felt the dance to be a natural way of honouring the powers that rule the world, since through it they, as it were, put themselves in tune with them. In this connection it is not irrelevant for me to mention a further passage from the work of Lucian which I have already quoted. He speaks of the piety of the Indians who do silent reverence to the dance of the sun in imitative movements: "When in the early morning the Indians make their adoration of the sun, they do not, as we do, think it sufficient merely to blow a kiss towards it, but, turning towards Helios at his rising, they do him honour in a dance, carried out in deep silence, which imitates the dancing of the god."[2]

To return, however, to this matter of astral mysticism, now so much a thing of the forgotten past, we get a reminder of it and of the intimations behind it, in a text that is both historically and psychologically of the greatest importance. It is that strange man Honorius Augustodunensis—who has so many curious things to tell—who here instructs us concerning the mysteries of the dance: "The 'choir' of those who chant the Psalter", he says, "obtained its name from the *chorea canentium*, the

[1] Philo, *Quis Rerum Divinarum Haeres*, 88 (Cohn–Wendland, III, p. 21, ll. 4–8).

[2] Lucian, *De Saltatione*, 17 (ed. cit., p. 150).—See on this: F. J. Dölger, *Sol Salutis*, p. 22–3, Münster, 2nd ed. 1925; H. Oldenberg, *Die Religion des Veda*, pp. 110 and 432, Stuttgart–Berlin, 1917.—Pliny the Elder, *Naturalis Historia*, VII, 2, 22, reports that the Indian fakirs (*philosophi*) stare at the sun all day.

singing and dancing chorus which in ancient times was used in the worship of idols; in this way, in their errors, people sought to praise the gods with their voices and to serve them with their whole bodies. What they sought to imitate in their dances was the rotation of the firmament, while with the joining of their hands they endeavoured to represent the intertwining of the elements. The sound of their singing was meant to recall the harmony of the planets as they made music together, the movement of their bodies stood for the motions of the constellations and the clapping of their hands and the stamping of their feet was meant to be as the noise of thunder." In so far as it is a part of idol worship Honorius will naturally have none of this, yet he is not unaware of the dim glimpse of truth that lies at the bottom of it, and he boldly continues thus: "The faithful have imitated these practices and transformed them into the worship of the true God. They still seek to make use of musical instruments when they dance because it is said that the heavenly spheres make a sweet melody as they circle through the skies." And in justification of such customs Honorius recalls the dancing of Miriam before the people of Israel when they had been freed from their bondage in Egypt, the dancing of David before the ark of the covenant, and Solomon's impressive ordering of the singers in his temple.[1]

This brings me to the attempts made by the Christians of antiquity to give the dance its sacral place and justisfication within the Christian mystery. Now, thanks to the excellently documented searches of J. Quasten,[2] it has undoubtedly been proved that, by and large, music and

---

[1] Honorius Augustodunensis, *Gemma Animae*, I, 139 (*PL* 172, 587 C f.).
[2] J. Quasten, *Musik und Gesang in den Kulten der heidnischen Antike und christlichen Frühzeit*, especially pp. 232ff., Münster, 1930.

the dance played no liturgical role in the ancient Church;
the Christian of the time was bound to look on such things
as manifestations of the detested pagan forms of religion
and as expressions of the pagan religious spirit. Indeed
Chrysostom leaves us in no doubt on the matter when in
one of his sermons he makes the forthright declaration
that "ἔνθα γὰρ ὄρχησις ἐκεῖ διάβολος – where there is
dancing there is the devil".[1] Yet this was not quite all.
There were, as we have seen, the biblical precedents for
a sacral dance, nor could the Christian quite forget the
feeling that in imitating the heavenly dance of the stars
he was in touch with some great cosmic secret, and
there was always the yearning based on something very
deep-seated in the human heart which made men long to
join in the shining choirs of the angels. And even if it was
not the dance mystery of the cosmos which he thus
penetrated, there were the measures of yet other dances
that came to the thoughtful Christian's mind—for he
knew that the Creation was not the only game played by
God, there was also the game of grace; and in this he
was called to play a part. There were the divinely sacred
dance steps of the incarnate Logos whom Hippolytus had
called the "leader of the mystical dance", that wonderful
"springing and leaping" of the Bridegroom as he hurries
towards his bride who is mankind. He read of this in the
Song of Songs: "Behold he cometh leaping upon the moun-
tains, skipping over the hills. My beloved is like a roe, or
a young hart" (Cant. 2. 8). Again it was Hippolytus who
brought these words into the context of the Christian
mysteries in a passage which mystical theologians were
to remember right into the Middle Ages. "O these great
mysteries!" he writes. "What is meant by this 'leaping'?

[1] John Chrysostom, *Homiliae in Matthaeum*, 48[49], 3 (*PG* 58, 491).

The Logos leapt from heaven into the womb of the Virgin, he leapt from the womb of his mother on to the cross, from the cross into Hades and from Hades once more back on to the earth—O the new resurrection! And he leapt from the earth into heaven where he sits on the right hand of the Father. And he will again leap on to the earth with glory to bring judgment."[1] Thus the images flow together. There are the memories of the ancient mysteries and of the dances that were a part of them; there are the dancing figures of the Bible and there are echoes of mystical allegories—and in all of these pious men dimly sense the great dance that moves before the eyes of God.

All these things tended to break down such inhibitions as the Christian might have felt towards the dance and to engender a more tolerant attitude. In one of his sermons Gregory Nazianzen recalls to his flock the dances of the ancient mysteries which have now been done away with: "But if you must dance, because you are a lover of feasts and festivities, then you may; but do not dance the dance of the shameless Herodias who brought death to the Baptist. No; dance the dance of David before the ark of God, for I believe that such a dance is the mystery of the sweet motion and nimble gesture of one who walks before God (τῆς εὐκινήτου καὶ πολυστρόφου κατὰ θεὸν πορείας εἶναι μυστήριον)".[2]

Here is a thought that is both Christian and Greek and the same can be said of some words of Gregory's

[1] Hippolytus, *In Canticum*, 11 (GCS I, 1, pp. 347–8). Thought and expression were borrowed from Hippolytus first by Ambrose, *Expositio Psalmi* 118, 6, 6 (*CSEL* 62, pp. 111–12) and *De Isaac vel Anima*, 4, 31EF (*CSEL* 32, 1, p. 661); from him they were taken over by Pseudo-Cassiodorus, *Expositio in Canticum Canticorum*, 2, 8 (*PL* 70, 1064B), Bede, *In Canticum Canticorum Allegorica Expositio*, 7 (*PL* 91, 1225D f.), and Paterius, *Expositio super Canticum Canticorum*, 11 (*PL* 79, 907B).
[2] Gregory Nazianzen, *Orationes*, V, 35 (*PG* 35, 709C).

friend and namesake from Nyssa. They are words spoken in a homily and recall Plotinus both in spirit and form. "Such a dance", he says, "really signifies a high tension of joy. . . . For it is a rhythmical motion of the body in which the inner disposition of the soul is made visible to the bodily eye; for man is of a dual nature and consists both of body and soul."[1] The true Christian should be a royal dancer like David before the ark of the covenant, and none should despise him as Michal his wife despised the dancing king.

Ambrose, slightly more cautious, interprets this biblical prefiguration as follows: "This servant played before the face of the Lord, . . . but his wife who found fault with such dancing was made unfruitful as a punishment and bore no royal child. . . . And if thou art still in doubt, hearken to the word of the Gospel. The Son of God says: 'We have sung to you and you have not danced' (Matt. 11. 17). The Jews were rejected because they did not dance and did not know how to beat time with their hands, and the heathen nations were chosen who gave God their applause in spiritual fashion. . . . For the dance that David danced is the glorious dance of the wise. And that is why in the lofty dance measures of the spirit he could mount to the throne of Christ where he beheld him and heard the Lord say unto his Lord: 'Sit thou at my right hand' (Ps. 109. 1)."[2]

For Augustine the dance of David is in a most profound sense symbolic. It is a "mystical figuration" of the sacred harmony of all the different sounds and gestures in the eternal peace of the city of God,[3] and

[1] Gregory of Nyssa, *Homiliae in Ecclesiasten*, VI, 4 (*PG* 44, 709CD).
[2] Ambrose, *Epistulae*, 58, 7–8 (*PL* 16, 1179f. [1230]).
[3] Augustine, *De Civitate Dei*, XVII, 14 (*CSEL* 40, 2, p. 245).

there were to be many others who approached the problem in much the same way. The German, Hrabanus Maurus, can still declare that the sacred dance is the symbol of "the devotion of an ever wakeful heart and of the pious agility of the limbs of the body".[1] We can now understand why, in the East also, the *Painter's Guide* of Mount Athos tells the artist to write on an ikon representing the Church as mother and bride: "O Church, rejoice in the Lord, make a glad noise and dance!"[2]

It is clear enough that up till now we have largely been dealing with an attempt to allegorize the dance. The fact is that through the dance and in other ways too the Muses were beginning to claim a place in cultic life and that this produced a counter-effort to sublimate such invasions on to a spiritual plane. But we are still faced with the question whether no sacred dance ever maintained a place in the actual liturgy of the Church. The Catholic liturgy, sustained as it is by chaste gesture and by movements so measured and slow that they seem to be weighed down by the very mysteries they are seeking to express—this Catholic liturgy is itself very like a single solemn piece of playing or miming. In such a setting the dance could surely not be looked upon as wholly out of place. Actually, however, the answer given by the expert is rather different from what such a consideration might suggest, and Dom Gougaud, who has made such dancing in churches the subject of considerable research, says quite unequivocally: "There is nothing to prove or even to render it probable that any kind of sacred dance was ever admitted into the liturgy of the Church either in anti-

---

[1] Hrabanus Maurus, *Commentarii in Matthaeum*, IV, 11, 2 (*PL* 107, 913A).
[2] *Malerbuch vom Berge Athos* (ed. G. Schäfer, p. 327).—Cf. P. Clemen, *Romanische Monumentalmalerei in den Rheinlanden*, p. 351, Düsseldorf, 1916.

quity or in the centuries that followed. In every age the dance was something that lay outside actual official worship."[1] For all that, however, this learned scholar is compelled to admit that in almost every century and in countless churches, a sacral dance, carried out both by clergy and laity, has been woven around the austere core of the liturgy. Moreover, in this flow of liturgical improvisation the boundaries between cultic and popular forms frequently disappeared. On feasts of martyrs the Christian of antiquity, in Greece and also in Africa, was often moved to give expression to his joy by performing a sacral dance at the graves of his heroes. The night vigil was filled on these occasions with both dance and song. The stern Fathers of the Church, who knew something of the pagan origin of such practices, puckered their brows, however. Caesarius of Arles, for instance: "*Ista consuetudo ballandi de paganorum observatione remansit* – This custom of dancing [during the vigils of the martyrs' feasts] is a survival of pagan practices."[2]

A hundred years before Caesarius' adjuration Augustine had preached a sermon in which with true pastoral zeal he had tried to lift his congregation's passion for the dance on to a spiritual plane. His words are so fresh and vivid that we can almost see the saint before us. The scene is the basilica of St Cyprian the martyr, in Carthage; the time, just after the abolition of these dances on feast-day vigils, a step that had obviously saddened these gay city Christians. "We no longer celebrate the games of demons," he says. "And yet," he continues, "it is written:

[1] L. Gougaud, "La Danse dans les églises", in *Revue d'Historie ecclesiastique* 15 (1914), pp. 1–22; 229–45.

[2] Caesarius of Arles, *Sermones* (formerly Augustine, Appendix, 265, 4 [*PL* 39, 2239], now) 13, 4 (*CC* 103, p. 67 =G. Morin, *S. Caesarii Opera Omnia*, I, p. 65, ll. 26–7).

'We have sung and you have not danced.' " How then do we stand in regard to this saying? Then he continues thus: "He sings who commands. He dances who obeys. What else is dancing but following sounds, with the motions of the body? . . . In our case dancing means changing the manner of our life." The martyr Cyprian was, according to Augustine, the leader in this dance. "When God called the tune, he hearkened and began to dance—not with the motions of his body but with those of his soul. He adapted himself to this good music, this new music, he followed it: he loved and he endured, he fought and he conquered."[1]

Yet the voices of the bishops died away. The staying-power of what might well be called a popular liturgy was greater than that of these ingenious but not too easily comprehensible attempts at spiritualization, and one detects a note of pastoral resignation in the words of a Greek preacher when he says on the feast of the martyr Polyeuctus: "χωρεύσωμεν αὐτῷ, εἰ δοκεῖ, τὰ συνήθη – Let us dance in his honour, if you really must, the accustomed dances."[2] Augustine may well have tried, as he did in another of his homilies, to dismiss the matter with a few brief and pungent words, insisting that "the martyrs did not go dancing to their death, but with prayers upon their lips",[3] but the tide was too strong for him, and the following verses of Paulinus of Nola, composed for the

---

[1] Augustine, *Sermones*, 311, 5–7 (*PL* 38, 1415f.).

[2] Text in R. Aubé, "Homélie inédite". Appendix to *Polyeucte dans l'histoire*, p. 79, Paris, 1882.—Cf. Quasten, *Musik und Gesang*, pp. 243–4; Gougaud, *La Danse*, p. 10.

[3] Augustine, *Sermones*, 326, 1 (*PL* 38, 1449).—Lists of the ancient Church's laws against liturgical dancing will be found in Quasten, op. cit., pp. 245–7, and Gougaud, op. cit., pp. 10–14. The latter includes the medieval period also.

Man at Play

feast of the martyr Felix of Nola, may refer to an actual festal practice:

> *Ferte Deo, pueri, laudem, pia solvite vota*
> *et pariter castis date carmina festa choreis,*
> *spargite flore solum, praetexite limina sertis.*[1]

(Give praise to God, O ye boys, redeem your pious vows
and strike up festal hymns with chaste dances too,
strew flowers upon the ground and adorn the doors
    with garlands.)

Who could help thinking here of one of those Catholic processions at Corpus Christi? Or of the boys who to this day perform their dance before the mystery of the altar in the cathedral at Seville? This may well be the last survival of a sacral dance in church.[2] This cultic dance of the "Seises" of Seville is almost certainly a mediaeval institution, and surely the remarks of Miss J. E. Harrison must be accounted as very extraordinary—though very typical of a certain school of comparative religion—when she declares that the dances of Seville are a survival from those once performed by the Curetes in Crete in honour of the infant Zeus. "Great Pan is dead," she says, "but his spirit still dances."[3]

The truth is of course that man in all ages, and particularly in southern Europe, has always been a natural dancer—that is to say a natural artist—and has sought to express, in the sacral domain as in any other, whatever was really alive within his soul. In the dim light of Seville's cathedral boys dance in groups of six (*seises*);

---

[1] Paulinus of Nola, *Carmina*, XIV, 108–10. (*CSEL* 30, pp. 49–50).
[2] On the liturgical dances of Seville cf. Gougaud, op. cit., pp. 243–5; bibliography, p. 243, note 3.
[3] J. E. Harrison, *Epilegomena to the Study of Greek Religion*, p. 26, Cambridge, 1921.

82

they perform their dance before God according to strict and sacred rules that have come down from time immemorial. The actual historical origins of this practice are really of very little importance. What matters is the sheer loveliness of this act of service to God by body and soul alike.

May I mention yet another such sacral dance play that delighted the hearts of the pious by its symbolism, especially in France, during the Middle Ages? I have in mind the dance and ball game that was carried out by bishop and clergy towards evening on Easter day in the bishop's palace or even in the cathedral itself. It was no less a scholar than Bachofen who, in his work on the mystical significance of the ball, remarked that "this ball game, carried out in the choir of the church on Easter day, betokens an attitude towards the immortality of a future heavenly existence which had been handed down by tradition and which continued under the authority of the new faith."[1] It must, however, be said that when, to substantiate his argument, he refers to a letter of Sidonius Apollinaris, he is seeking to construct a set of causal relationships which will not stand up to the test of modern research. Sidonius, in the passage in question, refers to the celebration of a feast in honour of the martyr Justus which apparently had attracted a huge crowd. After the night vigil and Mass in the morning the people enjoyed themselves by playing ball in the fields with the bishop and the younger clergy taking part.[2] But all this does not amount to a cultic or liturgical act and has nothing to do with the custom obtaining, as the evidence shows, in the Middle Ages and right down to the fourteenth century in a number of French cathedrals,

[1] J. J. Bachofen, *Urreligion und antike Symbole*, p. 480.
[2] Sidonius Apollinaris, *Epistulae*, V, 17 (*PL* 58, 548AB).

a custom which may, as Robert Stumpfl has shown, quite possibly represent an ancient Germanic Easter practice which had survived and forced its way into the sphere of worship itself.[1]

Let me, however, first review the actual known facts. On Easter day and during the so-called *libertas decembrica*, i.e. about the feast of the Holy Innocents or the New Year, it was the custom for the bishop and his clergy to play a ball game. This was done either in the courtyard of his palace or in the choir of the cathedral, a strict dance measure being followed. John Beleth gives us the following account: "There are also a number of churches in which it is the custom even for bishops and archbishops to play with their subordinates in their courtyards. They even condescend to play ball with them."[2] William Durandus gives us rather more detailed information for the thirteenth century: "On this day in various places the prelates play with their clergy, either in the cloisters or in the bishop's palace. They even condescend to play ball or to organize dances and singing. This is called 'December freedom' after the custom that once upon a time prevailed among the heathen, according to which slaves, herdsmen and serving girls were permitted a certain freedom during this month and could even give orders to their masters."[3]

The same kind of thing took place on the afternoon of Easter day. We possess a Ritual from Besançon for the year 1582 which gives the following directions for Vespers on that day: "After the ending of None the dances take place in the cloisters, or if the weather is wet, in the centre

[1] Robert Stumpfl, *Kultspiele der Germanen als Ursprung des mittelalterlichen Dramas*, Berlin, 1936.

[2] John Beleth, *Rationale Divinorum Officiorum*, 120 (*PL* 202, 123C).

[3] William Durandus, *Rationale*, VI, 86.

84

of the nave. During these are to be sung the chants found in the processional. And when the dance is ended drinks of red and white wine will be served in the chapter house."[1] We possess an even more exact account of this Easter custom in the case of the cathedral of Auxerre. There the dance, combined with a sacral ball game, took place in the cathedral choir and—so we are expressly told—upon the so-called "labyrinth" which decorated the floor in the form of a mosaic: *"choream circa daedalum ducentibus"*. To the melody and rhythm of the Easter sequence, *Victimae paschali*, bishop and clerks moved in a carefully regulated dance order over the pattern of the labyrinth, throwing a ball to one another. This deeply symbolic practice was given the name *pilota* which is the Latin word for this Easter ball.[2] It should be added that the custom of decorating the floor of the church with a labyrinth had already obtained in antiquity, and such labyrinths were called *daedala* after Daedalus of Crete, the first mythical designer of these things. The French name is *dédale*. In the Christian interpretation, the labyrinth was a symbol either of the *Sancta Ecclesia*, as is proved by the superscription at Castellum Tingitii (Orléansville) in Algeria,[3] or of the confusion of the world, from which one escaped after finding one's way through its devious patterns on the floor of the church. The superscription on the labyrinth in the church of St Sabinus in Piacenza, for instance, reads as follows:

> *Hunc mundum tipice Laberinthus denotat iste*
> *intranti largus, recedenti set nimis artus.*[4]

[1] Cf. Gougaud, *La Danse*, p. 235.
[2] Quoted in du Cange, *Glossarium Mediae et Infimae Latinitatis*, s.v. "Pelota".
[3] *DAGL*, VIII, col. 973–82, s.v. "Labyrinthe", Paris, 1928.
[4] Quoted *ibidem*.

85

(The labyrinth in symbol represents this world,
wide for him who is entering it, but too narrow for
him who would leave it.)

Moving in solemn dance step along the convolutions
of such a labyrinth, the bishop and the clerks of Auxerre
would throw the Easter ball to one another, rejoicing like
children in their redemption, for this was the evening of
the day which had celebrated the victorious sun of
Easter. We shall surely not be in error in supposing that
all this was a cultic development that had now taken on
Christian colours, though its origin was the Easter
ball game of the old Germanic tribes, for it is the con-
quering sun that the ball represents,[1] and, as I have
pointed out elsewhere,[2] the Christian feast of Easter is
the great day of Christ the sun which goes on its thundering and blazing way across the labyrinth of this earth.
The deep significance of this Easter dance of the clergy
of Auxerre is the same as that behind Hippolytus' great
Easter hymn of praise which had been composed a
thousand years before: "O thou leader of the mystic
round-dance! O divine Pasch and new feast of all things!
O cosmic festal gathering! O joy of the universe, honour,
ecstasy, exquisite delight by which dark death is destroyed . . . and the people that were in the depths arise
from the dead and announce to all the hosts of heaven:
'The thronging choir from earth is coming home.' "[3]

[1] Cf. R. Stumpfl, op. cit., pp. 136–7; E. K. Chambers, *The Medieval
Stage*, I, pp. 128–9, Oxford, 1903.—Further works bearing on the question
of liturgical dancing in the Christian Church are: G. R. Mead, *The Sacred
Dance in Christendom* (The Quest Reprint Series, II), London, 1926; Gillis
P:son Wetter, "La Danse rituelle dans l'Eglise ancienne", in *Revue d'histoire
et de littérature religieuses*, 1922, pp. 254–75.

[2] Cf. Hugo Rahner, "The Easter Sun", in *Greek Myths and Christian
Mystery*, pp. 103–29, London, 1963.

[3] Hippolytus, *Homiliae in Pascha*, 6 (*PG* 59, 744D f.).

We have come to the end of this enquiry into the theology of the dance. We may, therefore, return again to the beginning. All that pious men have sought to express in the dance by means of gesture and music is but a secret preparatory exercise for the object of their longing, the dance of everlasting life. What was lost by man at the beginning of the world is once more to be regained by him, and he is to know once again the blessed harmony of body and soul. There is no other image under which he can more eloquently describe the bliss of this everlasting life than under that of a heavenly dance. Plato shows in the *Phaedrus* that he has had an intimation of this; it is the passage in which he looks back from the travail of this earthly life upon the condition that has been lost and must be won back once more: "There we could contemplate shining beauty as in our happy dance we looked on the beatific vision and were initiated into a mystery that may be truly called most blessed, celebrated by us in our state of innocence, untouched by the evils which later awaited us, initiated to the sight of apparitions innocent and simple and calm and happy, which we behold shining in pure radiance, pure ourselves and not yet enclosed in that living tomb which we carry about with us now in the form of our so-called body in which we are imprisoned like an oyster in its shell."[1] Through all the works of the Greek devotees of this unbridled "spiritualism" we hear the echo of these words. Philo speaks of the "dance of the heavens whirling round the divine being";[2] Plotinus, of the "divinely-inspired dance that moves around the primal One";[3] Proclus and the

---

[1] Plato, *Phaedrus*, 250B.
[2] Philo, *De Praemiis et Poenis*, 20 (ed. Cohn–Wendland, V, p. 427).
[3] Plotinus, *Enneads*, VI, 9, 9 (ed. Harder, I, pp. 104–5).

Christian Areopagite join in this chorus.[1] In the initiation into the mysteries this heavenly dance is anticipated. We have in a fragment of Plutarch a description of the sense of being lost, of darkness, trembling and of sweating with fear, experienced by the candidate until, on an instantaneous transformation, he enters the heavenly fields where he hears singing and witnesses the dance of the initiates and may take part therein with a freedom that he is never again to lose; "μεμυημένος ἐλεύθερος ὀργιάζει."[2]

But the Christian who has overcome this "spiritualism" because of his faith in the resurrection of the body, knows that he will have part in that transformation and transfiguration of the body which St Paul referred to when he spoke of the σῶμα πνευματικόν (1 Cor. 15. 44), the spiritualized body—or, to use the language of the Fathers, a language that has the same pregnancy whether we think of it as poetry or theology: he will join the *chorus angelorum*, the dancing choirs of the blessed spirits.

Once more it was on an Easter day that Bishop Theophilus of Alexandria wrote the following words to his flock: "Let us then hasten to celebrate the festival of heavenly joy and join the choirs of angels where there are garlands of flowers, prizes and final victory, and where the palm-branches they had longed for are given to the triumphant",[3] and still today on the feast of a virgin the praying Church sings this of Christ:

---

[1] Proclus, *In Parmeniden*, VI, 57.—Dionysius, *De Caelesti Hierarchia*, VII 4 (*PG* 3, 232ff.), and see on this H. Koch, *Pseudo-Dionysius Areopagita*, pp. 170–1.

[2] Cf. Stobaeus, III, 52, 49 (Hense 1089).—Cf. Quarten, *Musik und Gesang*, p. 208.

[3] Theophilus, *Epistula paschalis*, preserved in Jerome, *Epistulae*, 98, 1 (*CSEL* 55, p. 185, ll. 12–14).

Qui pergis inter lilia
septus choreis virginum
sponsus decorus gloria.[1]
(Thou walkest among lilies,
surrounded by dancing choirs of virgins,
Bridegroom fair in thy glory.)

Thus heaven will be what was ours in the beginning—
Paradise.

Gregory of Nyssa has expressed this idea in his exegesis
of the heading to Psalm 52 in the Septuagint version:
"εἰς τέλος ὑπὲρ μαελέθ – Unto the end, for Maeleth."
This, he asserts, is a prophetic monition about the end of
time and Maeleth means "for the dancing chorus".
Thus the passage is telling us of the blessed dance that
will be ours at the end of days, even as it was in the
blessedness of Paradise. "Once there was a time when the
whole of rational creation formed a single dancing chorus
looking upwards to the one leader of this dance (πρὸς
ἕνα βλέπουσα τὸν τοῦ χοροῦ κορυφαῖον). And the harmony
of that motion which was imparted to them by reason
of his law found its way into their dancing." But original
sin destroyed this dance-like harmony of the spirit and
it is only εἰς τέλος, at the end of all things, that all will
again be as it was: "Our first parents still danced in
among the angelic powers. But the beginning of sin made
an end of the sweet sounds of this chorus. . . . Since then
man has been deprived of this communion with the
angels, and, since the fall, must sweat and most arduously
toil to do battle with and conquer the spirit that, thanks
to sin, now weighs upon him; but the spoils of victory will
be these: that which was lost in his original defeat will

[1] *Breviarium Romanum*, "Commune Virginum, ad Vesperas".

once more be his to enjoy, and once again he will take part in the dancing of the divine chorus. Thou hearest how to the words 'Unto the end' are added these others, namely: 'For the dancing chorus'. Be sure that under the form of a symbolic riddle thou art being warned not to succumb in the battle against temptation but to look steadfastly forward to the final victory. And this victory will come and thou shalt be found in the dancing ranks of the angelic spirits."[1]

[1] Gregory of Nyssa, *Homiliae in Psalmos*, 6 (*PG* 44, 508BD).

V

Eutrapelia: A Forgotten Virtue[1]

DID you ever practise eutrapelia? An odd question. Most of us have never even heard this strange Greek word, "eutrapelia", and scarcely anyone knows anything about the virtue which bears this name. But a person who is at all acquainted with the history of ethics and moral theology knows that eutrapelia is among the virtues mentioned in Aristotle's Nicomachean Ethics: it was there that Aquinas read about it and since then poor Eutrapelia has led a miserable existence in the standard books of moral theology, scantily adorned always with the same quotations that Aquinas knew, tired and reduced to a virtuous neutral attitude, upholding the mean in recreational play and joking.[2]

Let us try for once to remove the dust which has settled on this virtue. For it has the soft brightness of a noble and ancient gem, placed in the ivory bedecked cover of a Christian Gospel Book. It is a virtue of Greek *humanitas*, baptized in Christ. It is therefore neither antiquated nor a concept exclusive to the perpetually repeated Scholastic catalogue of virtues. If we contemplate it lovingly, we shall

[1] Quotations from Aristotle and Cicero are given in the Loeb translations. The Fathers and St Thomas Aquinas have been translated from the original language, in the light of Father Rahner's German renderings and abridgment.—*Translator.*

[2] Cf. *Salmanticensis Cursus Theologicus*, Lyons, 1679, III, pp. 785f.; O. Schilling, *Lehrbuch der Moraltheologie*, Munich, 1928, II, pp. 14, 350; B. H. Merkelbach, *Summa Theologiae Moralis ad Mentem D. Thomae*, Paris, 1938, II, pp. 980 f.; H. Noldin, *Summa Theologiae Moralis*, Innsbruck, 1952[20], I, p. 260.

receive an answer to secret and heart-stirring questions as to how we are to give a mature Christian character to our modern existence, thrust as we are into the midst of this evil (and yet so lovely) world, into this noisy, merry (because mostly so mortally sad) world, from which a Christian may not seek refuge by imagining himself to be above it all.

The question that perpetually arises in such a train of thought is: may a Christian laugh, when he has heard our Lord's warning, "Woe upon you who laugh now; you shall mourn and weep" (Luke 6. 25)? May a Christian go on merrily playing when a stern and strict choice has to be made for eternity? Is it right for him to relax, to ease the senses, when experience constantly reminds him how these same senses draw him down? All these are questions which the Fathers of the Church raised solemnly and seriously, which Aquinas tried to answer after mature and enlightened reflection, which were brought to a head in the bitter controversies between the Jansenists and the "devout humanists" with their ideas of a heaven on earth. They are questions which are raised in a completely new form today, when we are concerned with the thorny problem of the "Christian in the world", with discovering a mean between accepting and rejecting joyous, refreshing, relaxing things, between gravity and playfulness, crying and laughing. The Greeks knew and lived something of this ideal of the "serious-serene" man.[1] Great Christian thinkers adopted it and worked it up into the wise and lovely doctrine of "man at play" expounded in the previous four chapters. As eutrapelia has become largely a forgotten virtue it will pay us to look into the

[1] L. Radermacher, *Weinen und Lachen, Studien über antikes Lebensgefühl,* Vienna, 1947.

school of the Greek and Christian sages, in order to hear what it is all about. What we shall learn there can give us strength and comfort.

We shall follow the example of Aquinas and first look up Aristotle's Nicomachean Ethics.[1] In his fourth book, the Stagirite speaks of the balanced mean in which every virtue consists and in which alone it maintains its true character and maturity. He then shows how this relates to joking and playing as activities which are just as necessary as seriousness and hard work for the development of a genuinely human life:

> But life also includes relaxation, and one form of relaxation is playful conversation. Here, too, we feel that there is a certain standard of good taste in social behaviour, and a certain propriety in the sort of things we say and in our manner of saying them. . . . It is clear that in these matters too it is possible either to exceed or to fall short of the mean.

This mean Aristotle finds realized in the person who can be called "eutrapelos": the literal translation, "well-turning", shows at once what is meant. This person stands between two extremes, the description of which is particularly important as showing how Aristotelian ethics emerged from the cult and politics of the city-state—a description which Aquinas later took over. The one extreme is the "bomolochos", the poor wretch who hung about the altar of sacrifice in the hope of snatching or begging an odd bit of meat; in a broader sense, one who was ready to make jokes at every turn for the sake of a good meal and himself to be made the butt of cheap gibes. The opposite extreme was the "agroikos", the "boor", whose coarse

---

[1] IV, 14 (1128a).

93

stiffness was despised by the "asteios", the highly cultured Athenian citizen. Thus Aristotle says:

> Those then who go to excess in ridicule are thought to be buffoons and vulgar fellows, who itch to have their joke at all costs, and are more concerned to raise a laugh than to keep within the bounds of decorum and avoid giving pain to the object of their raillery. Those on the other hand who never by any chance say anything funny themselves and take offence at those who do, are considered boorish and morose.

The "well-turning" person stands out against both extremes:

> Those who jest with good taste are called witty or versatile—that is to say, full of good turns; for such sallies seem to spring from the character, and we judge men's characters, like their bodies, by their movements.

The philosopher sees a parallel in the development of Attic comedy, from the obscene ribaldry of the old to the refined wit of the new. The ideal is the man who practises eutrapelia, who observes the mean:

> The buffoon is one who cannot resist a joke; he will not keep his tongue off himself or anyone else, if he can raise a laugh, and will say things which a man of refinement would never say, and some of which he would not even allow to be said to him. The boor is of no use in playful conversation: he contributes nothing and takes offence at everything; yet relaxation and amusement seem to be a necessary element in life.

This refined mentality of eutrapelia is therefore a kind of mobility of the soul, by which a truly cultured person "turns" to lovely, bright and relaxing things, without losing himself in them: it is, so to speak, a spiritual elegance of movement in which his seriousness and his moral character can be perceived. The object of eutrapelia is play for the sake of seriousness, as Aristotle once described it in an unforgettable chapter of the tenth book of the Nicomachean Ethics:[1]

> It follows therefore that happiness is not to be found in amusements. Indeed it would be strange that amusement should be our End—that we should toil and moil all our life long in order that we may amuse ourselves. For virtually every object we adopt is pursued as a means to something else, excepting happiness, which is an end in itself; to make amusement the object of our serious pursuits and our work seems foolish and childish to excess: Anacharsis's motto, Play in order that you may work, is felt to be the right rule. For amusement is a form of rest; but we need rest because we are not able to go on working without a break, and therefore it is not an end, since we take it as a means to further activity.

This rather exclusive aristocratic ideal of mental refinement and culture, which was revived again by Cicero in his work, *De Officiis*, could not at first have much appeal to Christians. The notion of eutrapelia, as developed by Aristotle, is therefore not to be met with at all in the morality and asceticism of primitive Christianity. The reason for this may be found already in the fact that in the language of late antiquity "eutrapelia" had acquired very different overtones. "Eutrapelia" had almost become "bomolochia" and to describe a person as "eutrapelos"

[1] X, 6 (1176b).

was to make him an object of contempt as a smart but garrulous windbag. Martial, for instance, gave to a clumsy and incompetent barber the nickname "Eutrapelos" to bring out the contrast.[1] It is evident that Aristotle's teaching had been forgotten.

Moreover, the Christian in the light of revelation had become more perceptive of the dangers of the "world", abandoned to evil and under the dominion of Satan. How then could anyone want to be "hot for the world"? Thus the word which once had so sublime a meaning entered into the language of the New Testament with all the encumbrances imposed upon it by the linguistic development of Koine and the stern world-renunciation of the primitive Church.

Paul warns his Christians in the Epistle to the Ephesians (5. 4) to avoid "ribaldry (*morologia*) or smartness in talk (*eutrapelia*)". It must always be a question of linguistic tact as to how we translate "eutrapelia" in this verse, but that it has a pejorative sense is already clear from the fact that Paul makes it equivalent ("or") to the chatter of fools. That is precisely how Jerome later understood it[2] and the Vulgate, as we know, translates it as "scurrilitas": namely, the vice of the *scurra*, the clown, the eternally jovial windbag. No: from the New Testament there was nothing to be done for Aristotle's Eutrapelia.

Clement of Alexandria, the first indeed to attempt to find an exact balance between Christian seriousness and a serene acceptance of the world, applies the word in the Pauline sense only when he is warning Christians against

[1] *Epigrams* VII, 83.

[2] *Comment. in Ep. ad Ephesios* III, 5 (PL 26, 520). On the exegesis of the Pauline "eutrapelia" cf. F. A. von Henle, *Der Ephesierbrief des heiligen Paulus*, Augsburg, 1908, pp. 259 f., and W. Bauer, *Griechisch-deutsches Wörterbuch zu den Schriften des neuen Testaments*, Berlin, 1952⁴, Coll. 592 f.

using "jocose (*eutrapela*) and unbecoming words" at their social gatherings.[1]

The Greek and Latin Fathers of the early Church were in fact always faced with the task of educating the naturally light-hearted and witty Christian, the product of the civilization of late antiquity, in the seriousness of Christian behaviour. We can understand it therefore when Ambrose, for instance—incidentally, wholly in the spirit of his model, Cicero—gives a warning against being too nimble in joking and playing, even though this appears in an address mainly to his clergy on whom he wants to impose the ancient Roman and Christian discipline:

> Joking should be avoided even in small talk, so that some more serious topic is not made light of. "Woe upon you who laugh now; you shall mourn and weep" (Luke 6. 25), saith the Lord: are we then looking for something to laugh at, so that we may laugh now but weep hereafter? I maintain that not only loose jokes, but jokes of any kind must be avoided—except perhaps when our words are full of sweetness and grace, not indelicate.[2]

We can see him, dignified and stern, this Bishop of Milan, presenting to his clergy his own ideal of Roman-Christian rectitude, with that episcopal solemnity which made the hypersensitive Augustine also feel that he was unapproachable:

> The pleasures of the table, of playing and joking, break down manly dignity and seriousness. Let us take care, when we are seeking mental relaxation, not to

---

[1] *The Tutor* II, 7, 53, 3 (*GCS*, Clement I, p. 189, 27).
[2] *De Officiis* I, 23, 103 (*PL* 16, 54 f.).

97

dissolve all the harmony, the concord—so to speak—of our good works.[1]

What Ambrose said to the clergy the equally strict Chrysostom preached to the people of Constantinople and Antioch, whipped up in every nerve with the lust for pleasure in the great city. We may read on this subject the sixth homily on Matthew's Gospel which the "Golden Mouth" delivered in Antioch in 390. Here we find ourselves in a world such as we have to reckon with today, in the gay city with its enticements to junketing, night life and unchastity disguised as merry-making.

> This world is not a theatre, in which we can laugh; and we are not assembled together in order to burst into peals of laughter, but to weep for our sins. But some of you still want to say: "I would prefer God to give me the chance to go on laughing and joking." Is there anything more childish than thinking in this way? It is not God who gives us the chance to play, but the devil.[2]

These are harsh words; and they were not forgotten. Aquinas returns to the question. The preacher of penance has to exaggerate, for he knows that men are always more inclined to follow their pleasant bent towards baser things and that in this way alone he can establish a balance: thus nothing is more exposed to easy-going and deceptive indulgence than the sensitive mean of true eutrapelia. Aristotle felt this indeed, when he observed that the "bomolochos" was also frequently called "eutrapelos", the clown a wit, because the comic is enormously popular

[1] *De Officiis* I, 20, 85 (*PL* 16, 49B).
[2] *Commentary on Matthew*, Homily 6, 6 (*PG* 57, 70D).

and most men are more enthusiastic about joking and ridicule than is fitting.[1]

It is of the greatest interest to see how, in the history of the christianization of the Greek eutrapelia, Aquinas made use of the material at hand from Aristotle and the Fathers of the Church. First of all then he interprets the above-quoted chapter from the fourth book in his commentary on the Nicomachean Ethics in this way:

> There is some good in playing, in as much as it is useful for human life. As man needs from time to time to rest and leave off bodily labours, so also his mind from time to time must relax from its intense concentration on serious pursuits: this comes about through play. Hence Aristotle says that man obtains in this life a kind of rest from his anxieties and preoccupations in playful conversation.... Those who go to excess in merry-making he calls *bomolochoi*, that is, "temple-plunderers", like the birds of prey who hovered about the temple in order to snap up the intestines of animals offered in sacrifice. So these people are always ready to seize anything which they can turn to ridicule. Such men are a nuisance through their efforts at all costs to raise a laugh.... But he says also that those who do not want themselves to make a joke and are annoyed by those who do, because they feel insulted, appear to be "agrii", that is, "boorish" and hard, because they are not softened by the pleasure of play.[2]

Here then the ancient doctrine of the Stagirite comes in a broad and full stream into a Christian book. Play and joking take their place in Christian morality; eutrapelia

[1] IV, 14 (1128a).
[2] *In decem libros Ethicorum Aristotelis ad Nicomachum*, lib. iv, lect. 16.

as the virtue of the mean here gains entry into moral theology and into asceticism.

Thus Aristotle shows what is the mean in playing. He says that those who exercise moderation in play are called *eutrapeloi*, "well-turning" (*bene vertentes*), because they are able to turn aptly into laughter what is said or done.

That is finely put: therefore the Christian may play; therefore also smiling, laughing, is a virtue. Here the way is prepared for the medieval theology of the merry Christian who sees the limits and inadequacy of all created things and for that very reason can smile at them: he knows the blessed seriousness of things divine. A person who does not understand this belongs to that class of whom Aquinas has aptly said: *non molliuntur delectatione ludi*, "they are not softened by the pleasure of play".

What is here presented mainly as an interpretation of Aristotle's text is developed by Aquinas in some illuminating pages of the second part of the *Summa Theologica*, where the question is raised: "Can there be a virtue in play?" Answering in the affirmative, Aquinas appeals to Augustine who at one time—still under the platonic influences of the early years of his conversion—spoke of relaxing the mind through play.[1] He discusses the severe words of Ambrose and Chrystostom of which we have already heard. It may help us to understand the clear teaching of Aquinas if we set out this article in a literal if somewhat abridged translation.[2]

First: It seems that there cannot be any virtue in play. For Ambrose says: " 'Woe upon you who laugh

[1] *De Musica* ii, 14 (*PL* 32, 1116A).
[2] *Summa Theologica* II–II q. 168 a. 2.

now; you shall mourn and weep,' saith the Lord. I maintain then that not only loose jokes, but jokes of any kind, must be avoided."

Second: Virtue is what God effects in us and without our co-operation. But Chrysostom says: "It is not God who gives us the chance to play, but the devil." Therefore there can be no virtue in play.

Third: Moreover, the Philosopher says that "the activities of play are not directed to any other end". But for virtue it is necessary deliberately to act for the sake of something else. Therefore there can be no virtue in play.

But against this we have what Augustine says: "I want you to spare yourself. For it befits a wise man to relax from time to time, to stop being intent upon the things he has to do." But such relaxation is obtained by joviality in words and deeds. Therefore, to indulge in these from time to time is fitting to the wise and virtuous man. The Philosopher also regards "eutrapelia" as the virtue which is exercised in play: we might speak of "gaiety" (*jucunditas*) or of "ready adaptability" (*bona conversio*).

We must then answer: Man needs bodily rest, so that the body can be revived: he cannot go on working without interruption, since he has limited powers which are adapted to certain definite tasks. The power of the soul is likewise limited, adapted to certain activities. If, then, he imposes on himself an undue strain through some of his activities, he feels the effort and becomes tired. This is because the body also co-operates in the activities of the soul, since the soul—even the intellect— uses powers which operate through bodily organs. But sensible goods are connatural to man. Hence, when the mind is raised above sensible objects, because intent upon the operations of reason, there arises out of this a certain mental fatigue. . . . Thus man becomes more fatigued in mind, the more unreservedly he devotes himself to the activities of reason.

As bodily fatigue, then, is relieved by resting the body, so mental fatigue must be relieved by giving rest to the soul.

But, as we explained when dealing with the passions, the soul finds its repose in pleasure. Therefore, as a remedy against fatigue of soul, we must provide some pleasure, drawing the mind away for a time from its absorption in thought. So we read in the Conferences of the Fathers that some were scandalized to find the Apostle John playing with his followers. John told one of them, who was carrying a bow, to draw an arrow: he did this several times and John then asked whether he could keep on doing it without interruption; the reply was that the bow would break in the end. John therefore argued that man's mind would also break if the tension were never relaxed.

Sayings and deeds of this kind, in which nothing more is sought than the soul's pleasure, are known as playing and joking. It is therefore necessary to make use of them from time to time to provide repose for the soul. That also is what the Philosopher says: "Life includes relaxation, and one form of relaxation is playful conversation." From time to time then we must make use of some of these things.

In this respect, however, three things are to be avoided. First and most important, this pleasure must not be sought in immoral and harmful deeds or words. Hence Cicero says (*De Officiis* I, 29): "There is a kind of jest which is coarse, rude, vicious, indecent." Secondly, we must take care not to lose entirely gravity of soul. Hence Ambrose says: "Let us take care, when we are seeking mental relaxation, not to dissolve all the harmony, the concord—so to speak—of our good works"; and Cicero: "As we do not grant our children unlimited licence to play, but only such freedom as is not incompatible with good conduct, so even in our jesting let the light of a pure character shine forth." Thirdly, as in all other human actions, we must see to it that play and joking are suited to the person, time and place, and duly related to other circumstances, so that (as Cicero also expresses it) they are "worthy of the time and the man".

Therefore, there can be a certain virtue in play. The Philosopher calls it "eutrapelia" and says that a person is "eutrapelos", "well-turning", because he is well able to turn deeds or words into relaxation.

In answer to the first objection, therefore, we must say: It has already been observed that joviality must be suited to the circumstances and the persons. This is particularly important in regard to sacred doctrine, which is concerned with matters of the greatest import. It is from this field that Ambrose wants to exclude joking, not from human life altogether.

In answer to the second objection, we must say that Chrysostom's words are to be understood of those who are excessively addicted to play and especially of those who make pleasure in playing the whole meaning of life. They are described in the Book of Wisdom (15. 12): "They have counted our life a pastime." Against this attitude, Cicero writes: "Nature has not brought us into the world to act as if we were created for play or jest, but rather for earnestness and for some more serious and important pursuits."

In answer to the third objection, we must say that the activities of play as such are not directed to an end beyond themselves. But the pleasure derived from these activities provides a certain relaxation and repose for the soul. Therefore, in moderation, we may indulge in play. As Cicero again says, "We may, of course, indulge in sport and jest, but in the same way as we enjoy sleep or other relaxations, and only when we have satisfied the claims of our earnest, serious tasks."

That is the teaching of Aquinas on eutrapelia in joking and playing. May our reflections on the subject affect us as his own thought affected him when, in the next article of the *Summa*, he recalled wistfully an incident in the Lives of the Fathers and thus touched on a lovely and profound mystery of the grace of God which "plays" in the world: "It was revealed to Paphnutius that a certain joker would be his companion in heaven."[1] And in the same article, Aquinas had the courage—astounding at that time—to open the Christian gates also to actors, to the art of the theatre and to all their patrons, as did later the gentle Francis de Sales.[2]

In our opinion, this is again the time to think out afresh the forms and scope of true eutrapelia. Not everything in our civilization is in the hands of the devil and thundering from the pulpit is not always in place. Just because so many "bomolochoi" are active in our world and slip into the obscenities of ancient Attic comedy, we Christians are not obliged to become "agroiki", but must try to realize the

[1] *Ibid.*, a. 3 (*Vitae Patrum* viii, 63: *PL* 73, 1170).
[2] *Introduction to the Devout Life* I, 23.

Christian ideal of the serious-serene human being at play in his fine versatility, in eutrapelia, in that serene abandonment to the seriousness of God which, according to Theodor Haecker, lies very deep in the foundations of European-Christian civilization.[1]

[1] See above, p. 35.